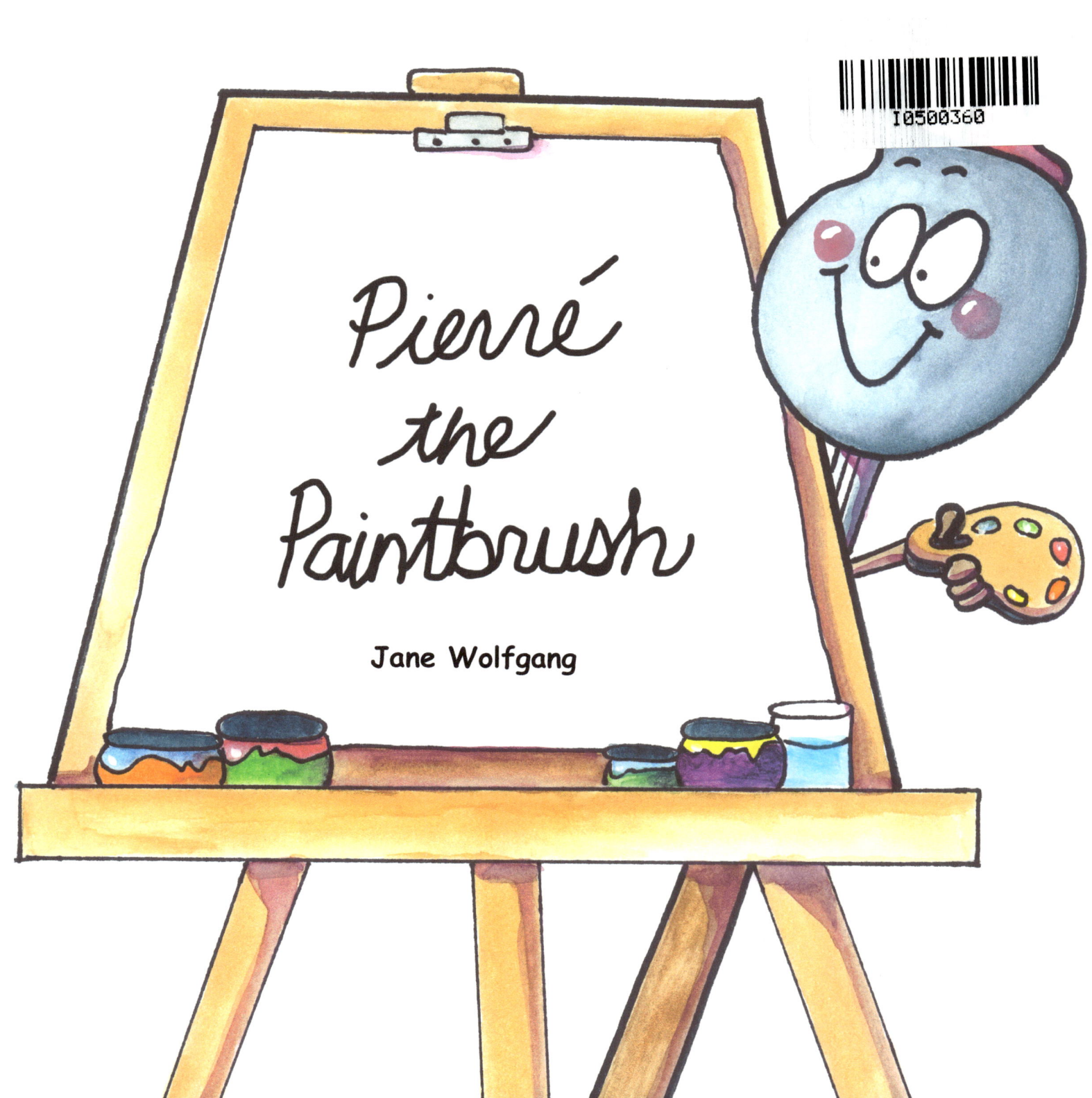

Pierré the Paintbrush

Jane Wolfgang

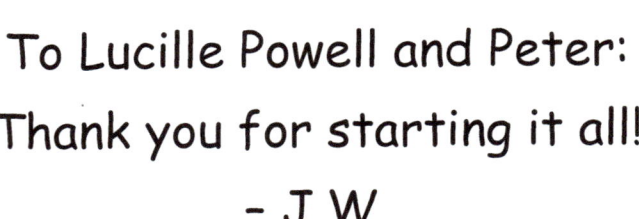

To Lucille Powell and Peter:
Thank you for starting it all!
– J.W.

Summary: Meet Pierré the Paintbrush as he teaches the fundamentals of painting and how to care for a paintbrush. This silly story provides kids with some helpful painting tips so that the process is both fun and educational.

ISBN-13: 978-1511947657
ISBN-10: 1511947659

CreateSpace, Charleston, SC

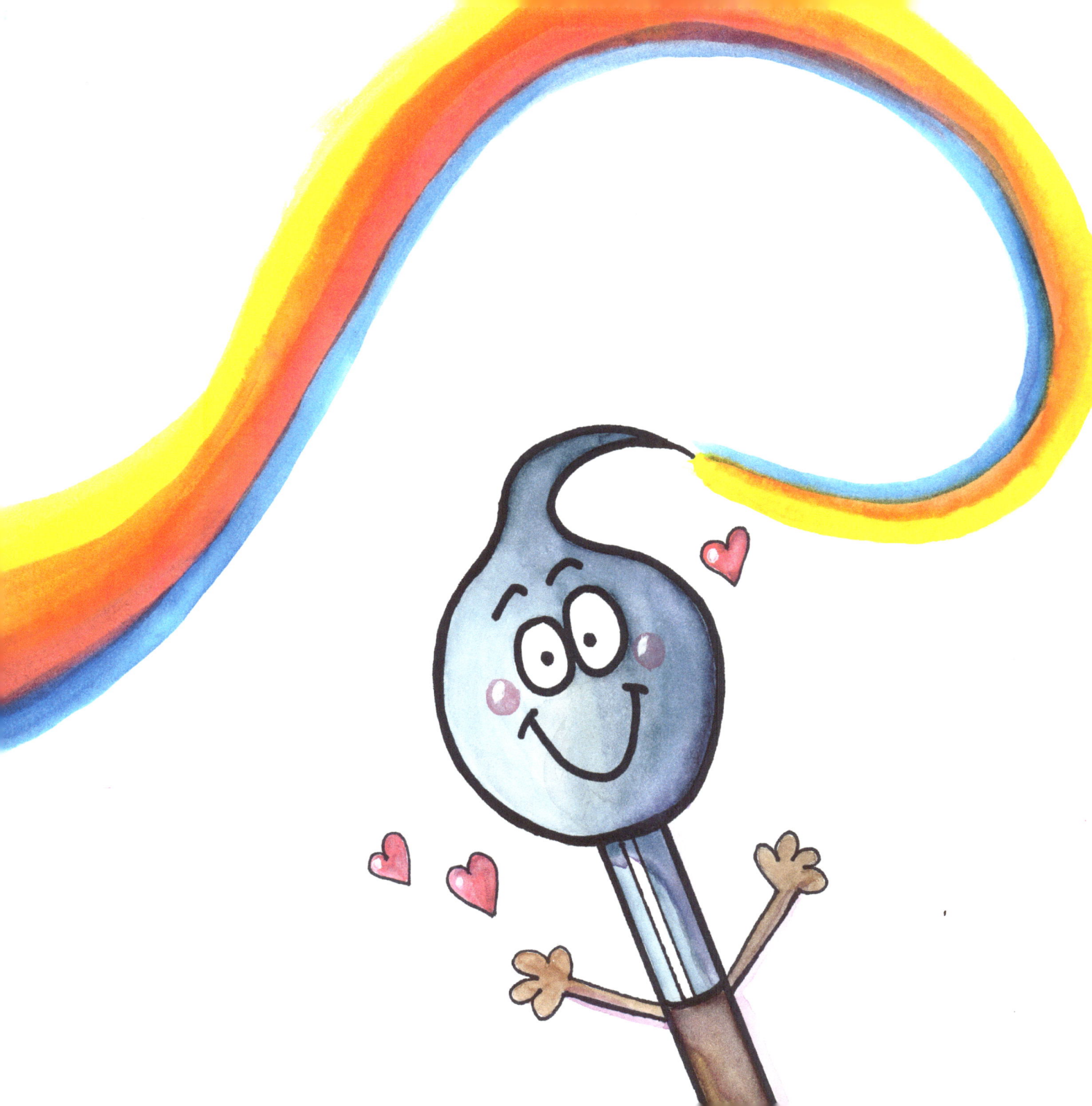

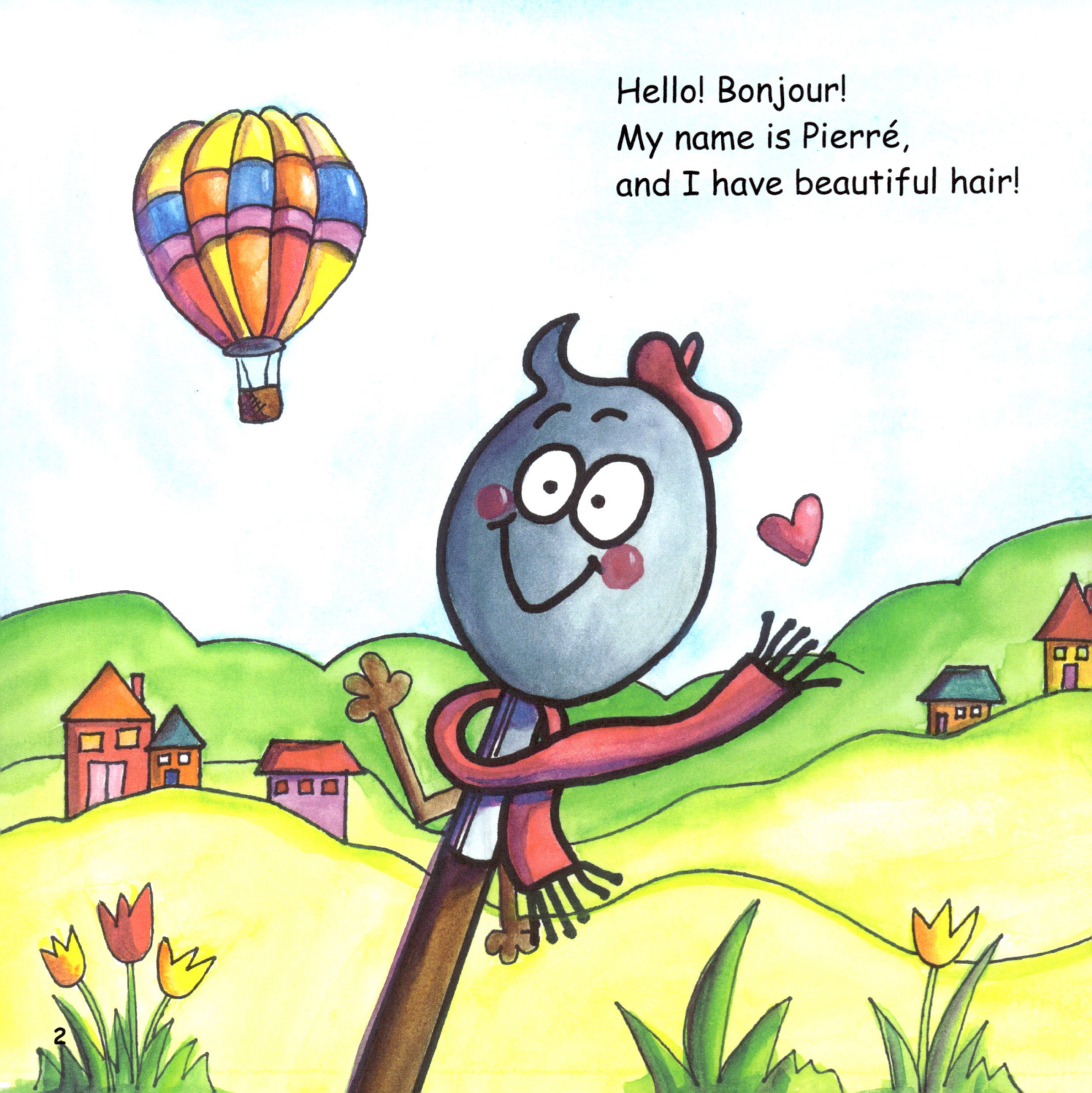

Hello! Bonjour!
My name is Pierré,
and I have beautiful hair!

2

Painting is what I love to do,
and I would like to paint with you!

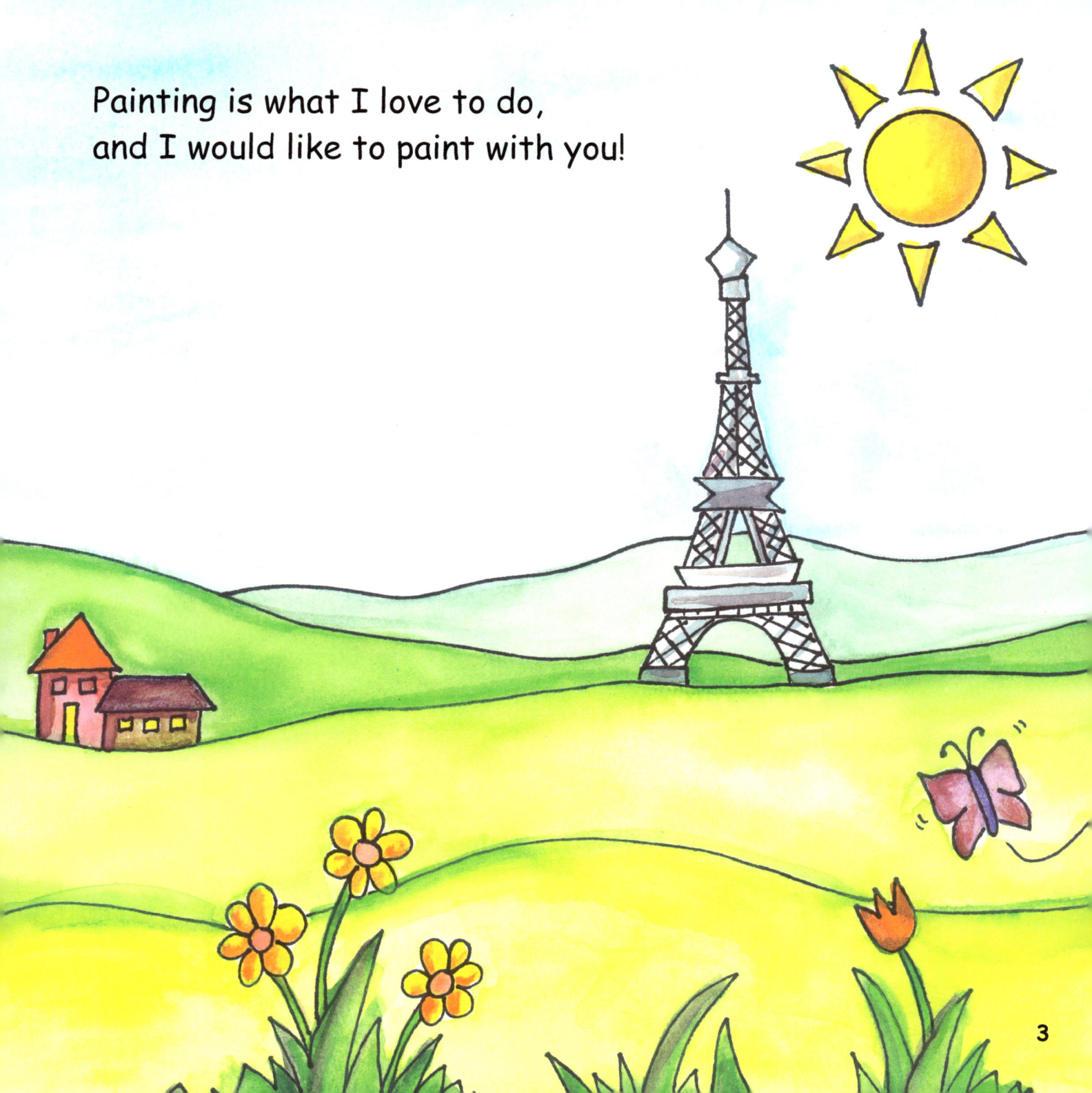

Would you like to paint with me?
For I am a paintbrush, I hope you see!

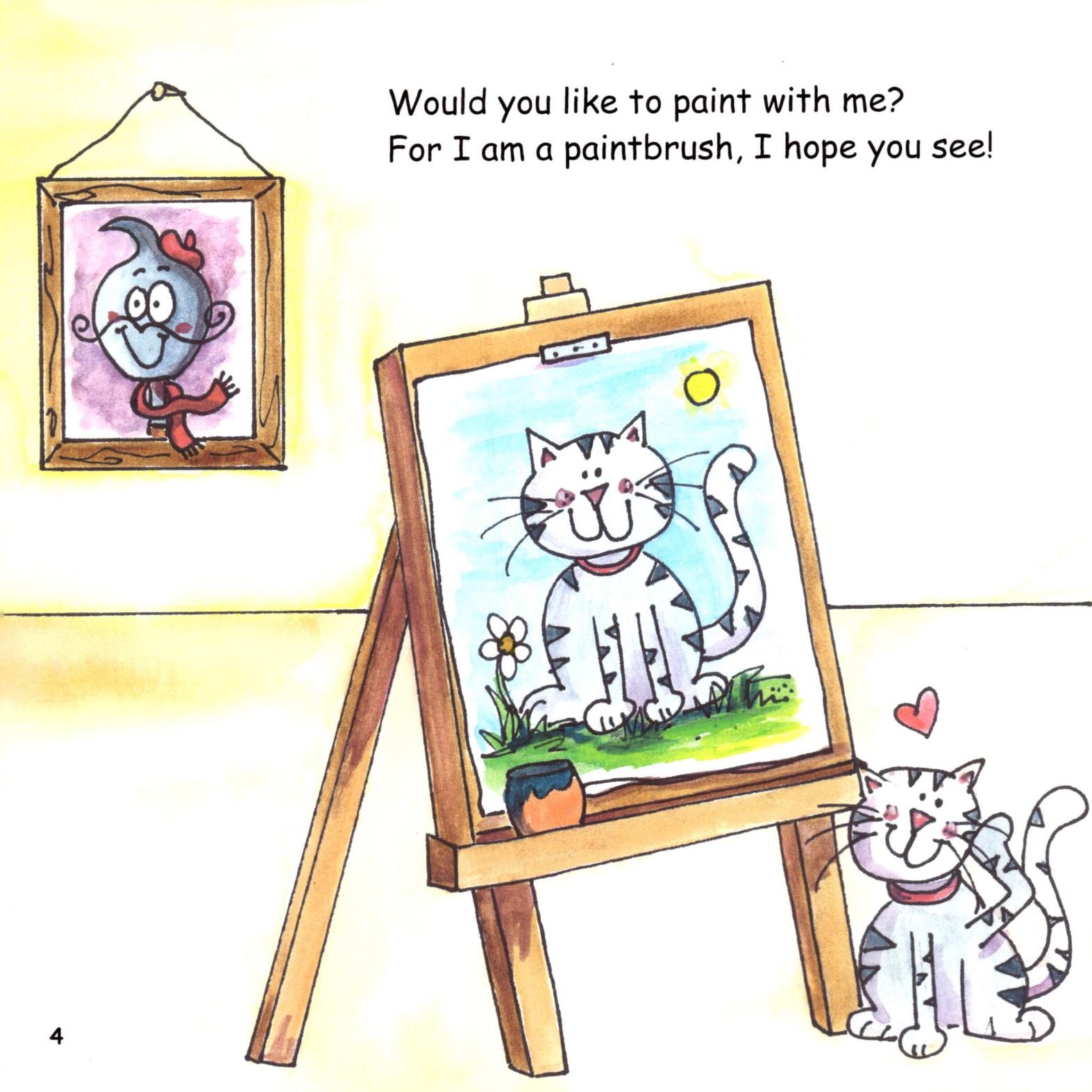

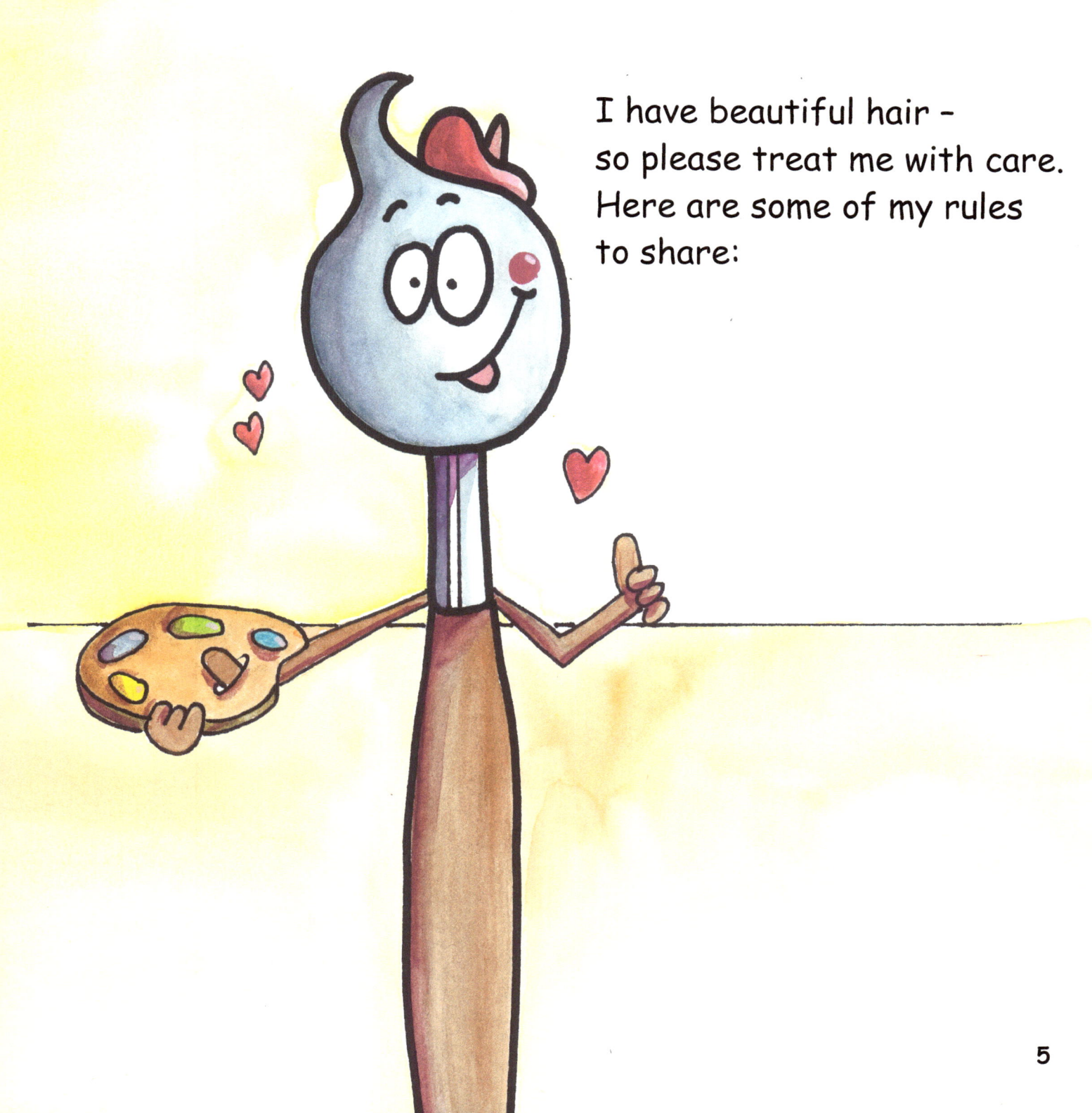

I have beautiful hair –
so please treat me with care.
Here are some of my rules
to share:

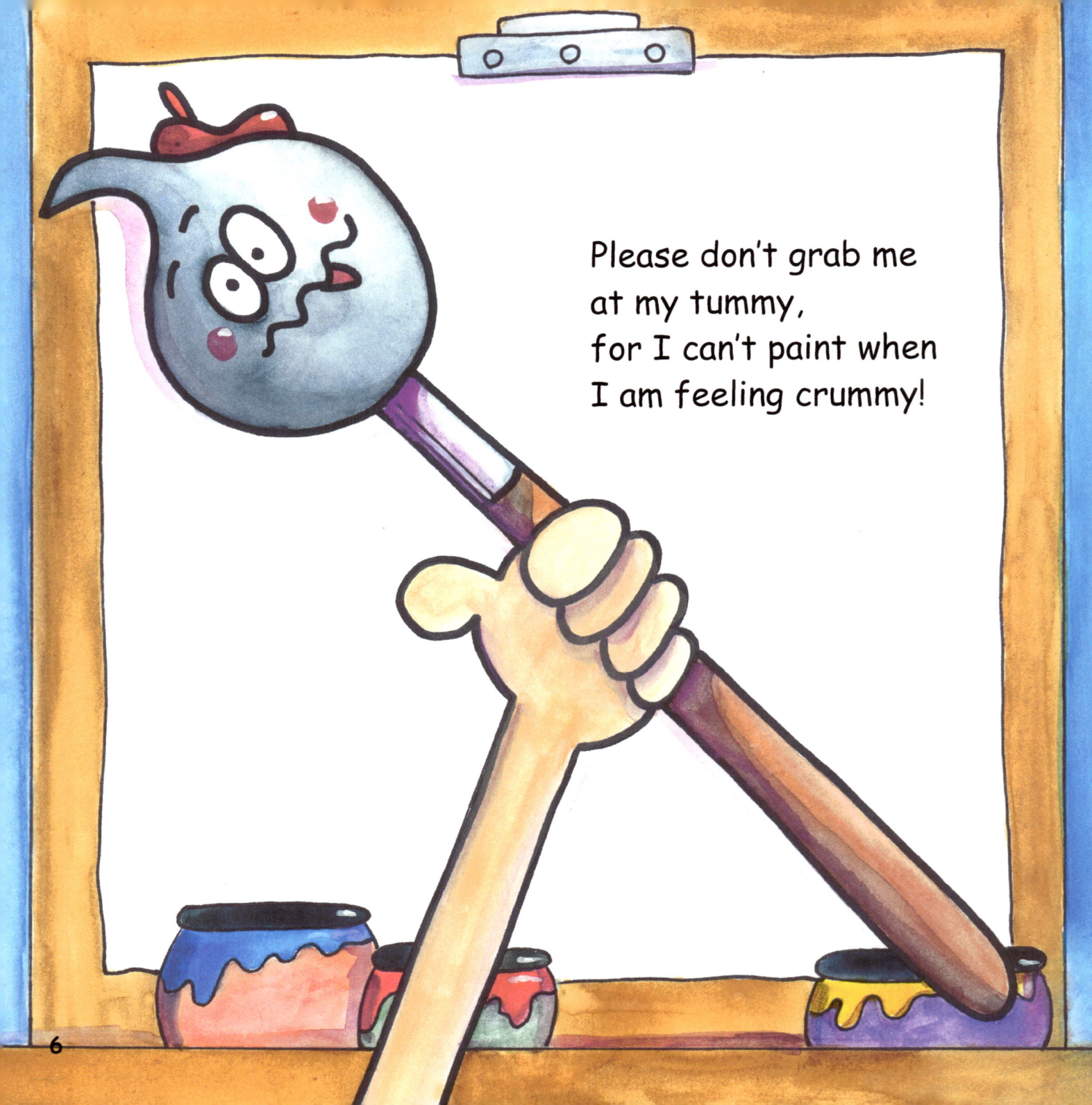

Please don't grab me
at my tummy,
for I can't paint when
I am feeling crummy!

6

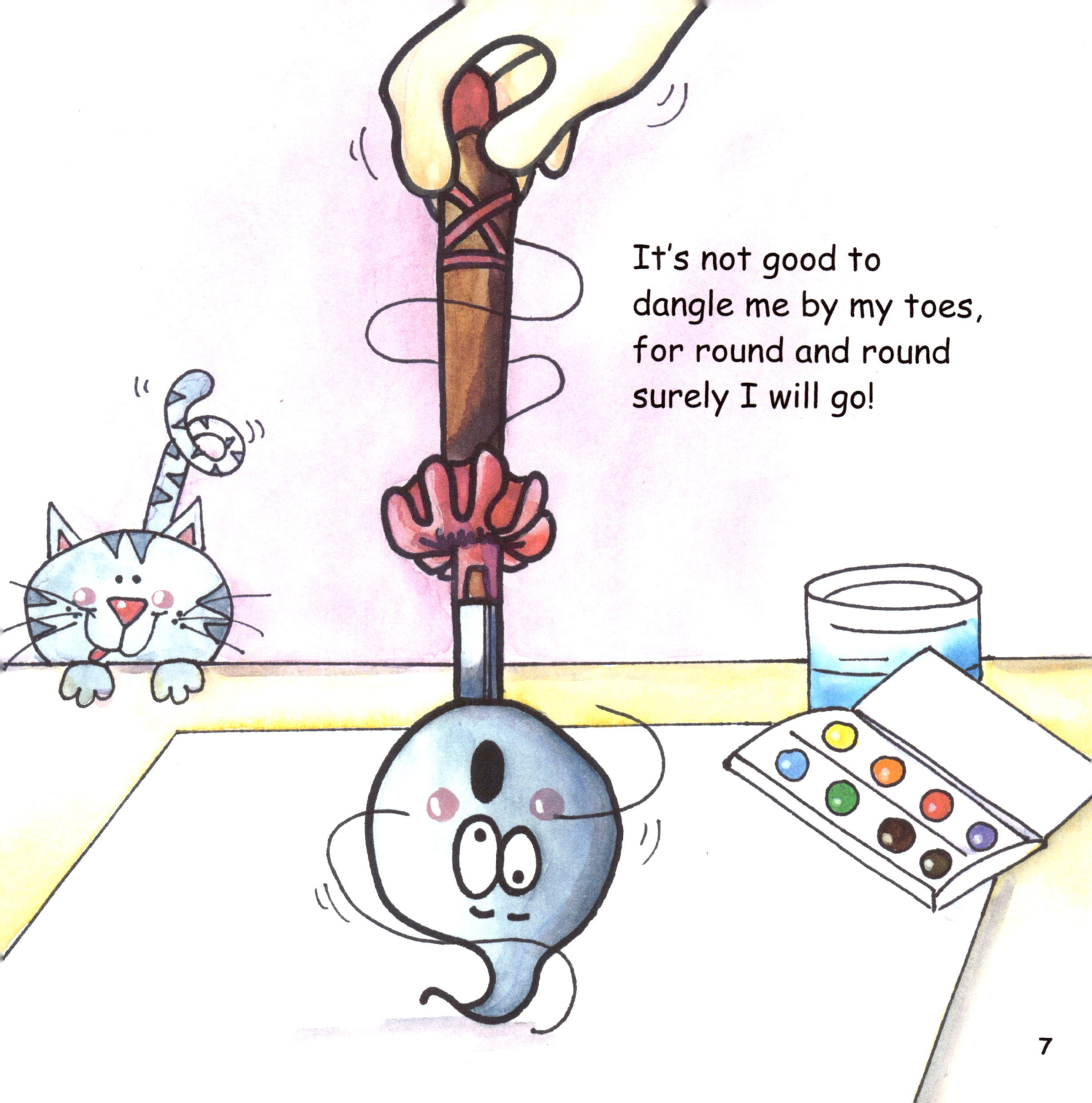

It's not good to
dangle me by my toes,
for round and round
surely I will go!

7

Please be careful not to
hold me so tight,
holding me like
a pencil – is just right!

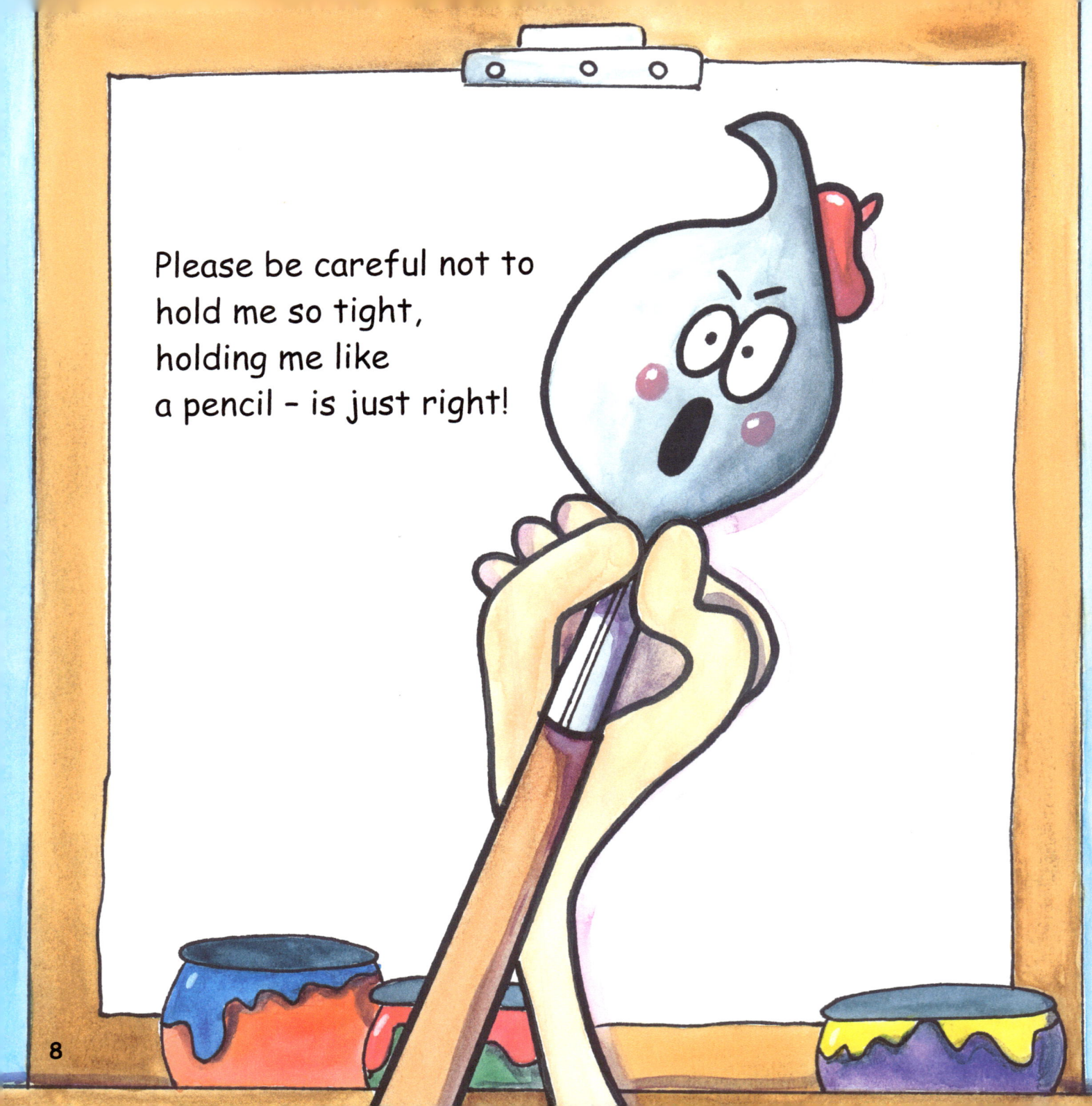

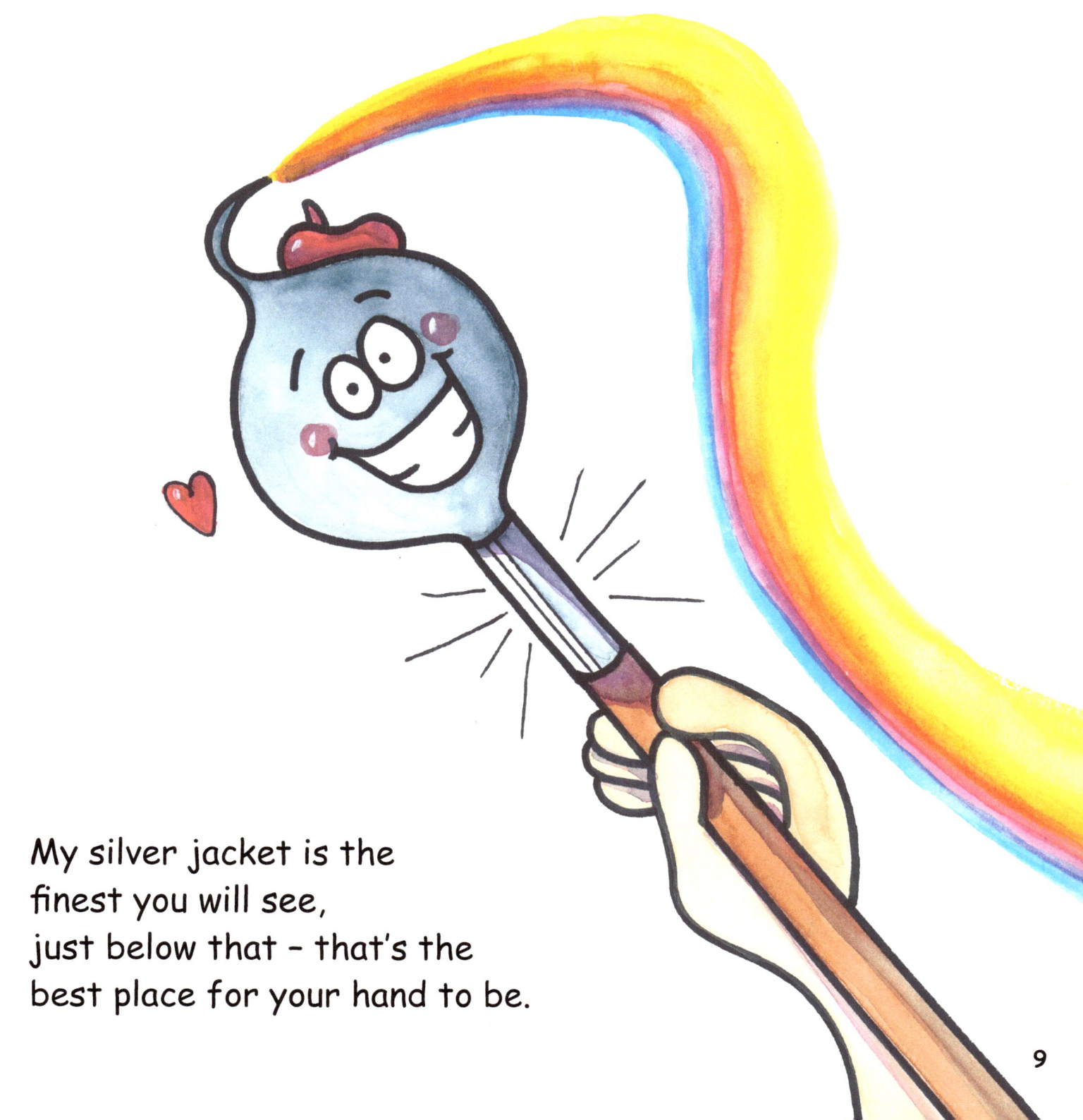

My silver jacket is the
finest you will see,
just below that – that's the
best place for your hand to be.

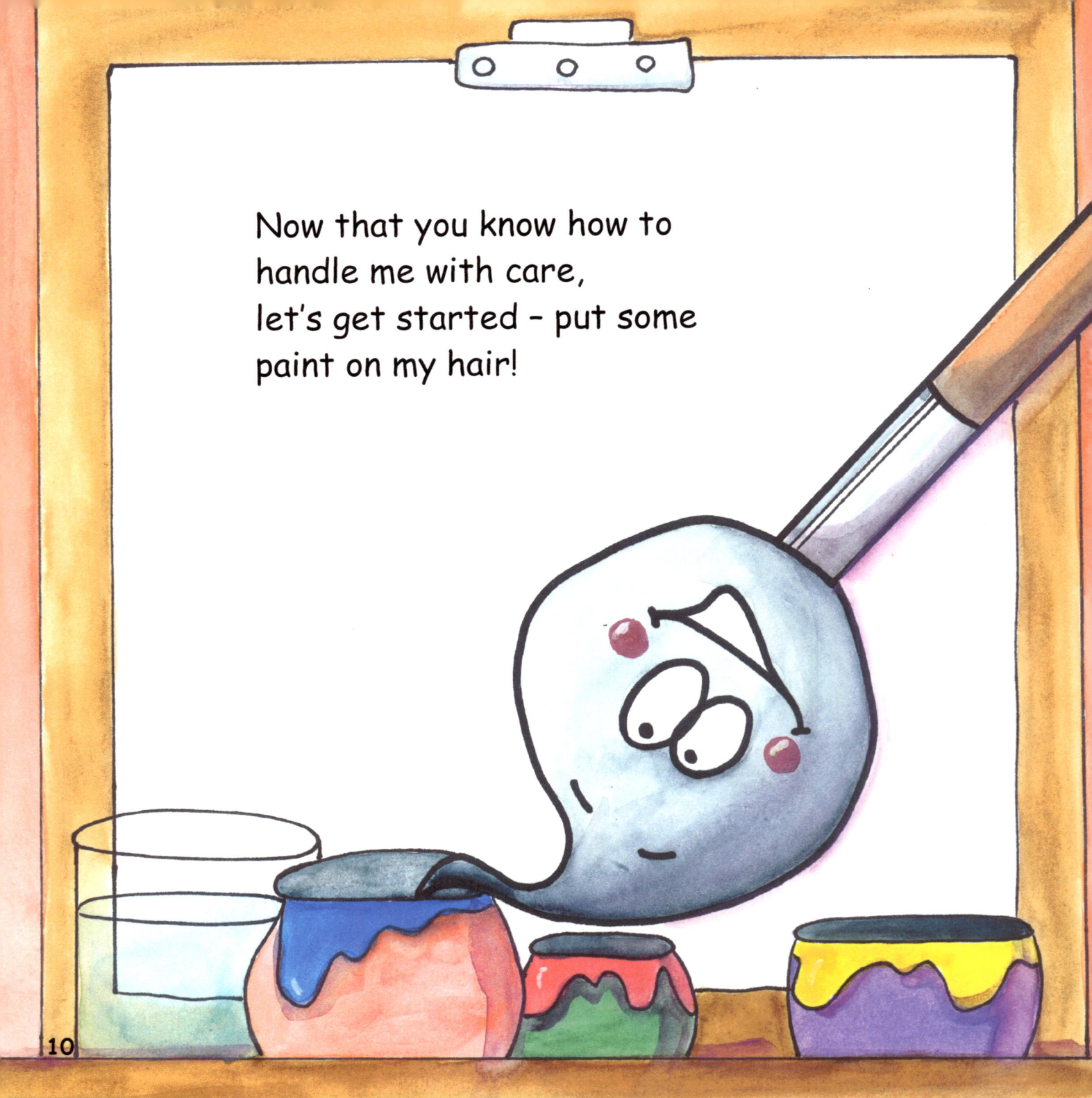

Now that you know how to
handle me with care,
let's get started – put some
paint on my hair!

Stop! No wait!

What are we going to paint?

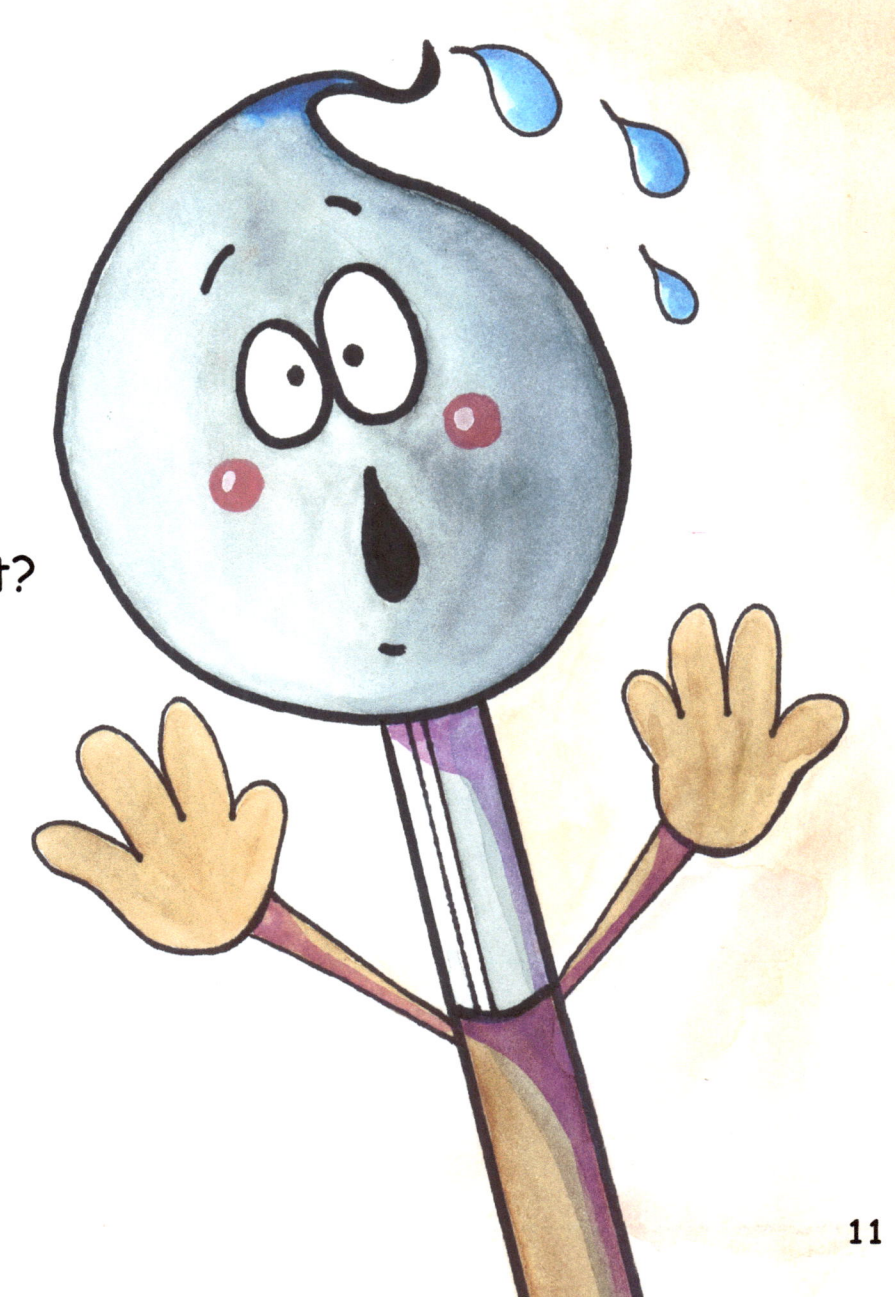

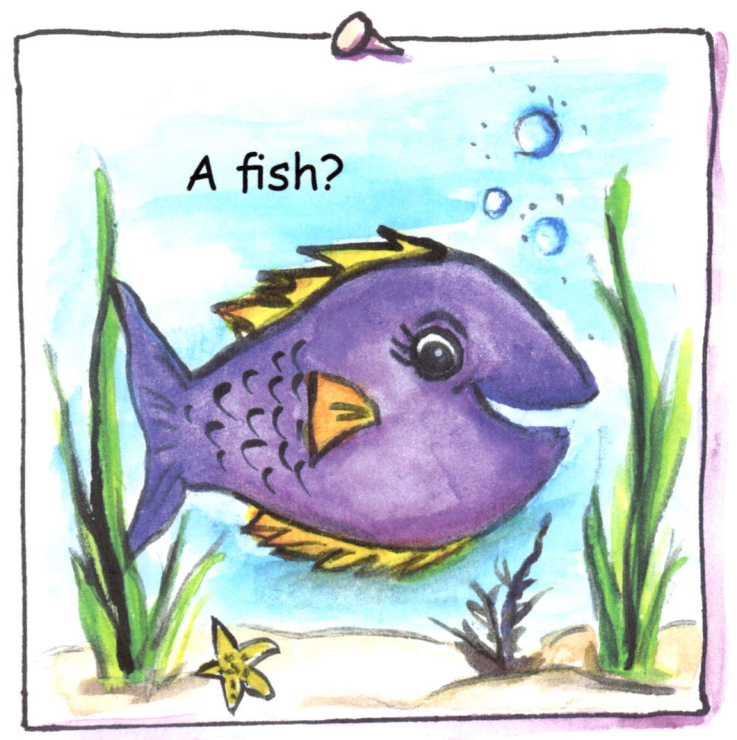

A fish?

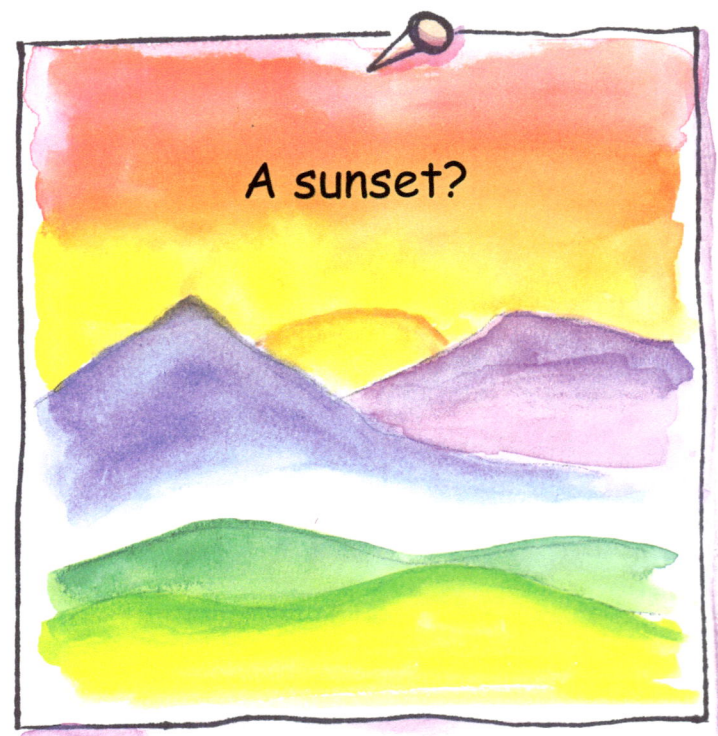

A sunset?

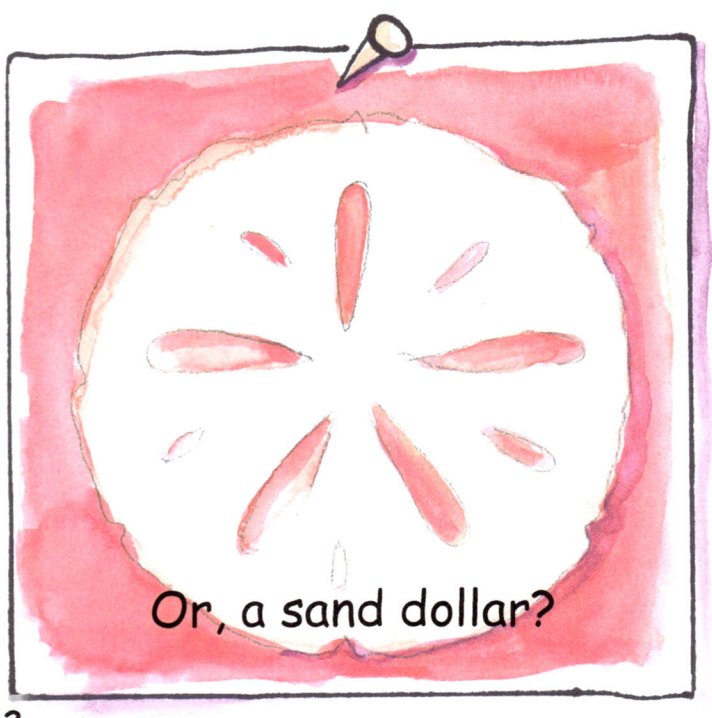

Or, a sand dollar?

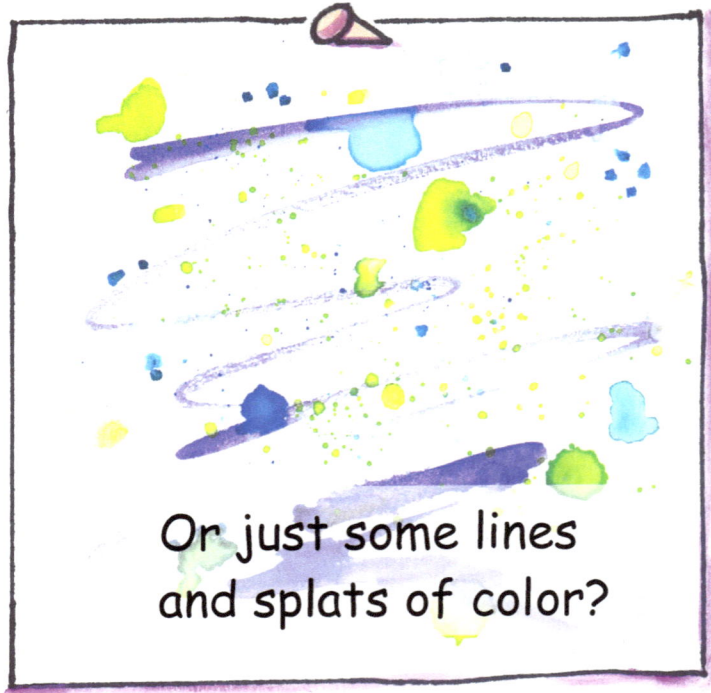

Or just some lines and splats of color?

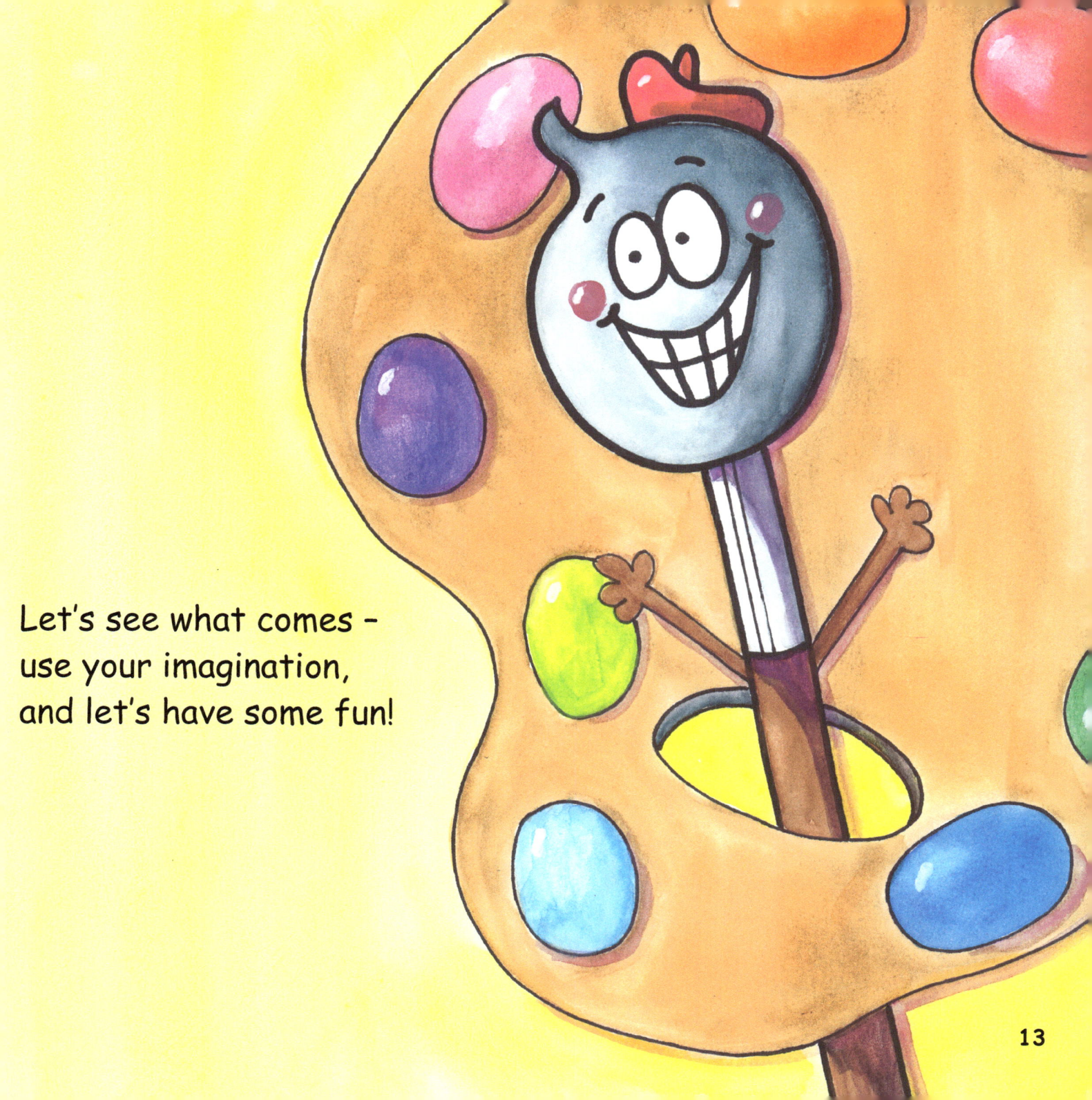

Let's see what comes –
use your imagination,
and let's have some fun!

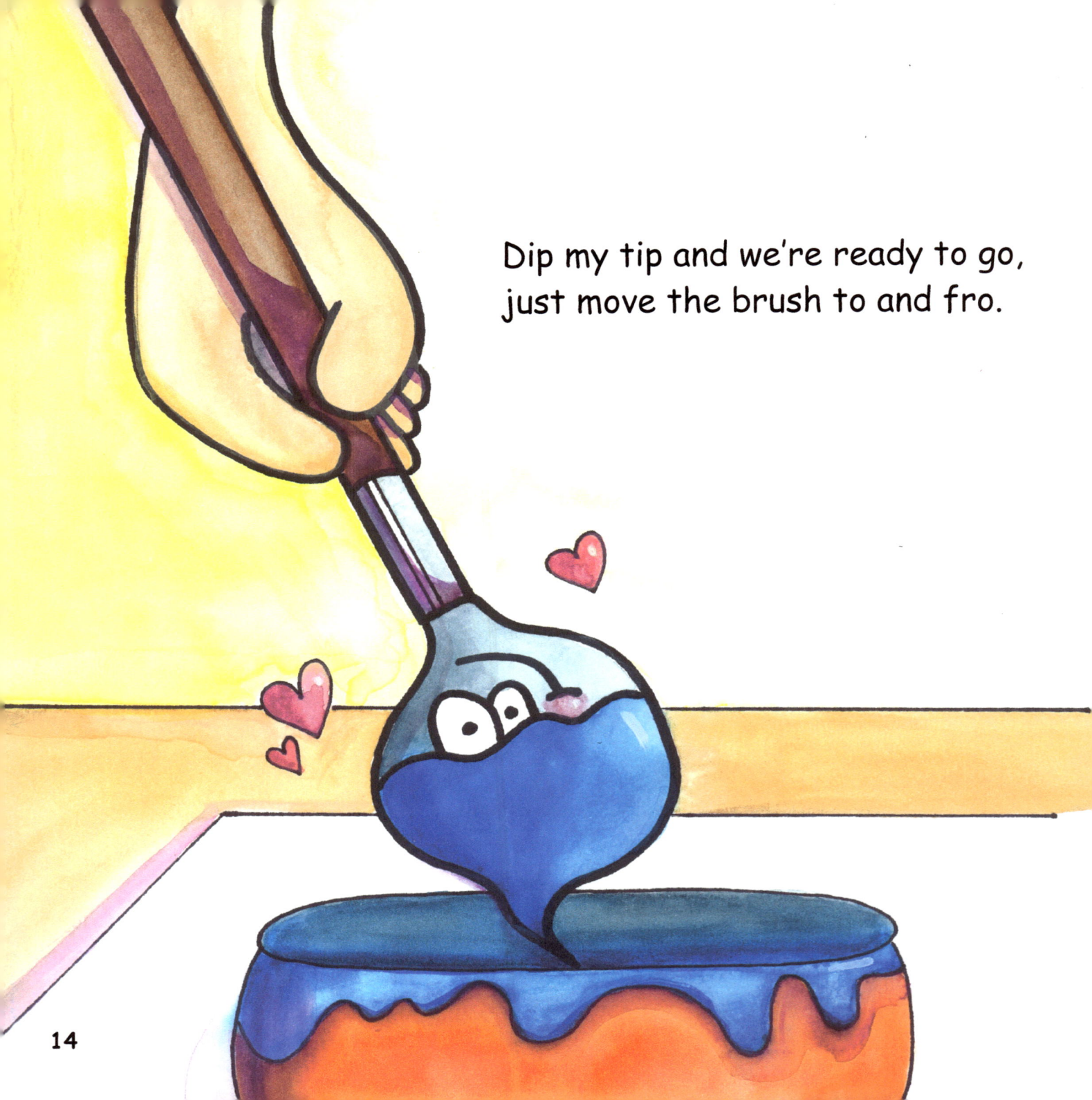

Dip my tip and we're ready to go,
just move the brush to and fro.

14

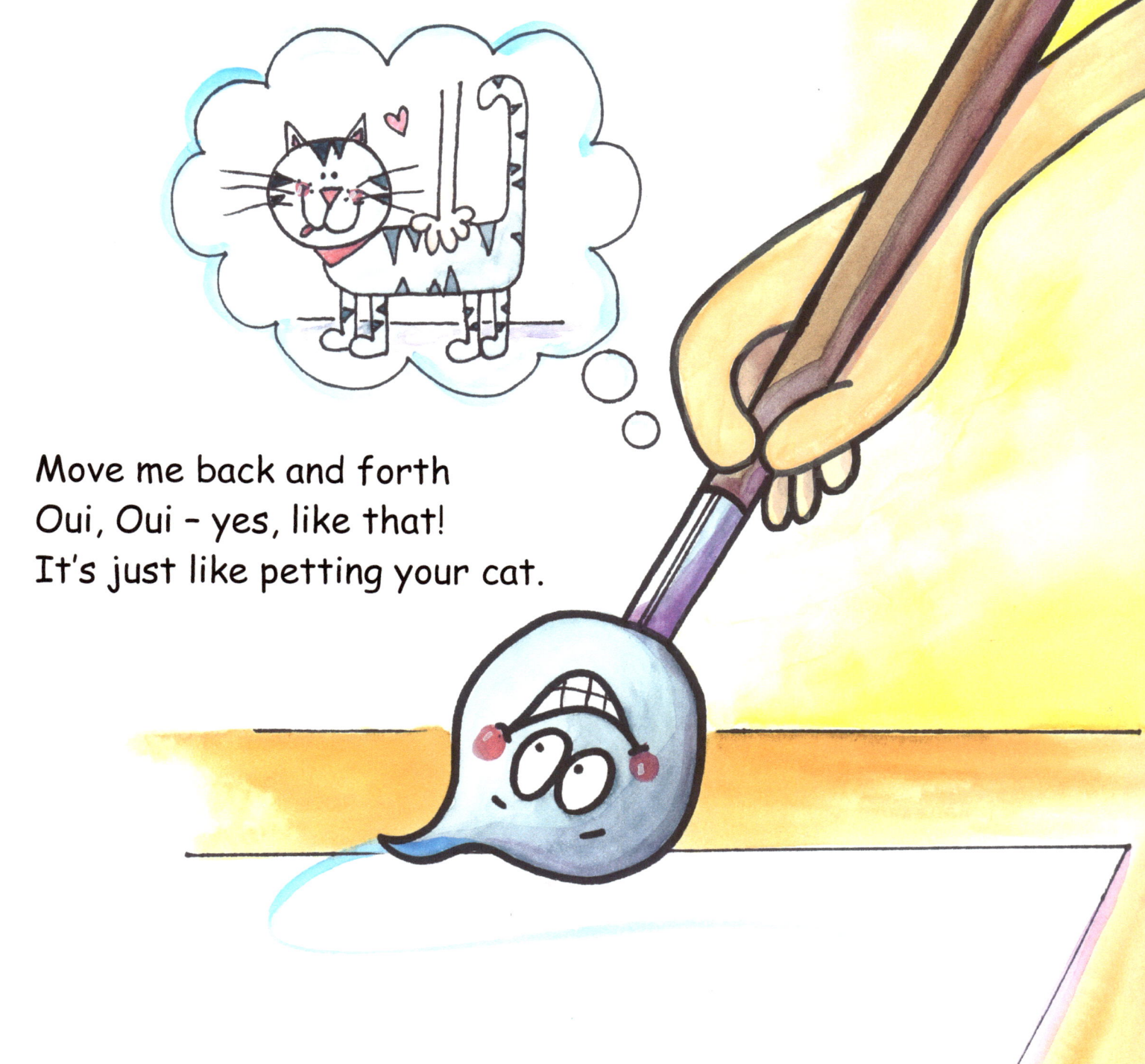

Move me back and forth
Oui, Oui – yes, like that!
It's just like petting your cat.

15

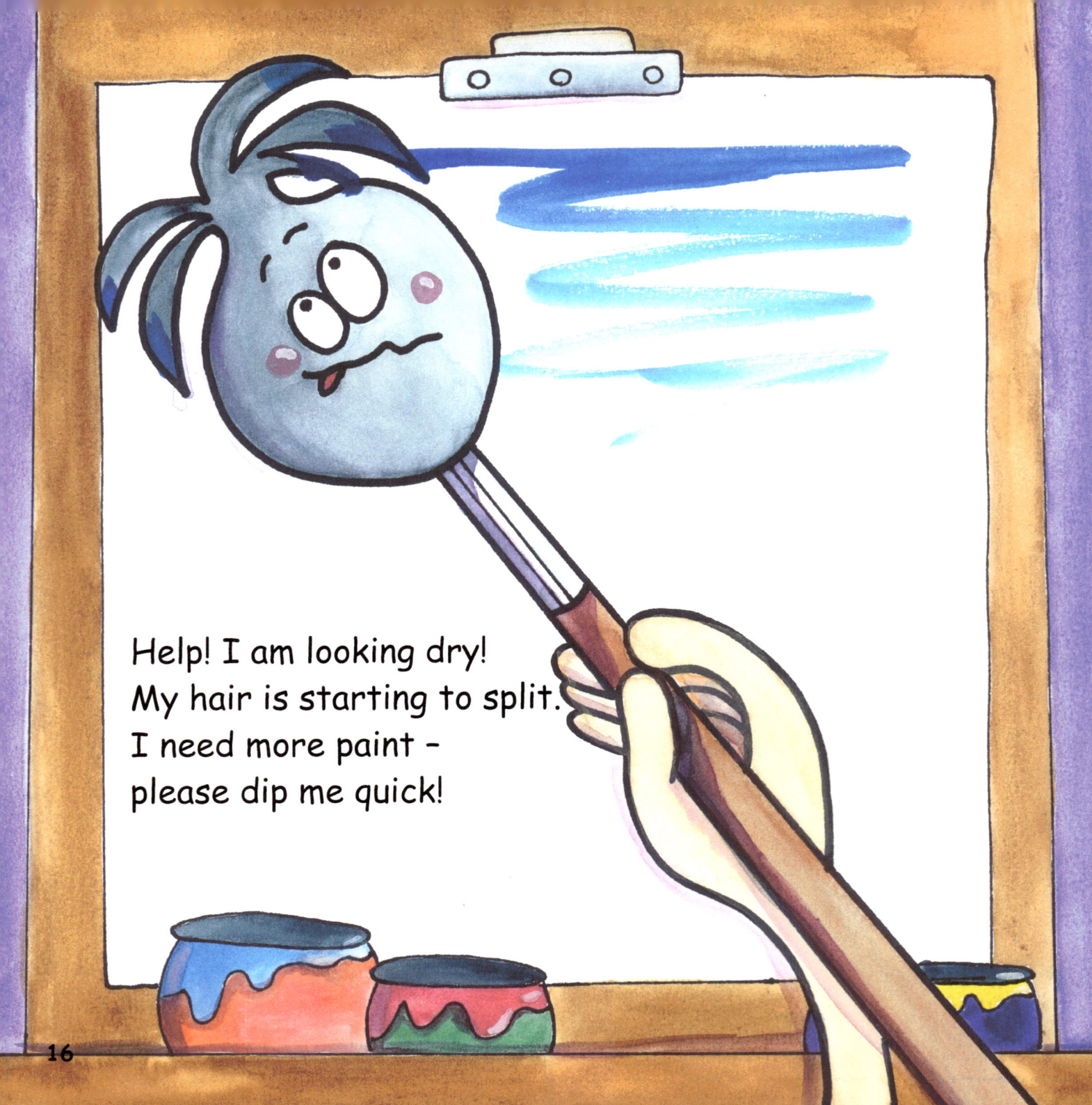

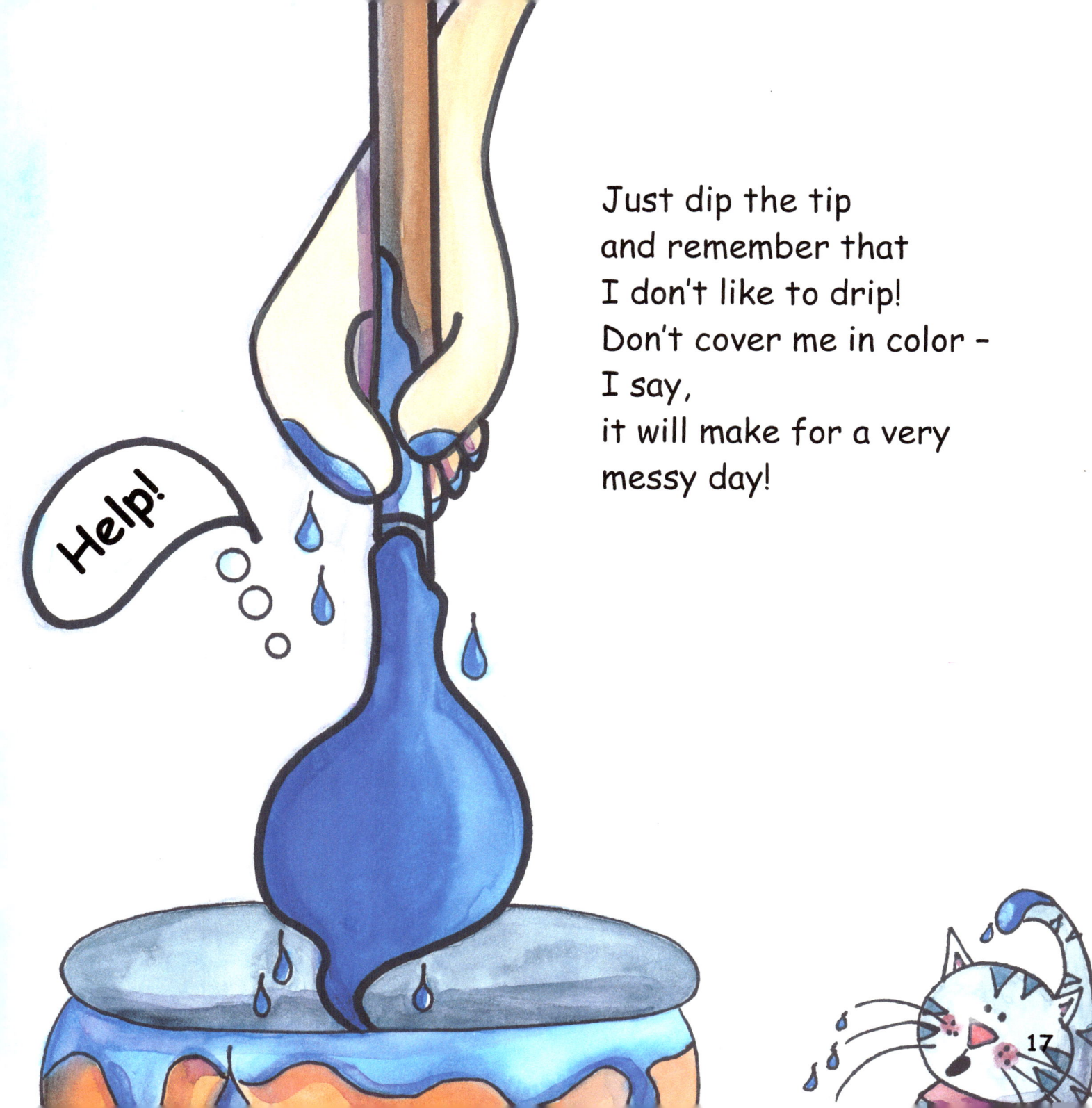

Just dip the tip
and remember that
I don't like to drip!
Don't cover me in color –
I say,
it will make for a very
messy day!

17

Please don't
mess up my
hair with
scrubbing –
just give my hair
lots of loving.

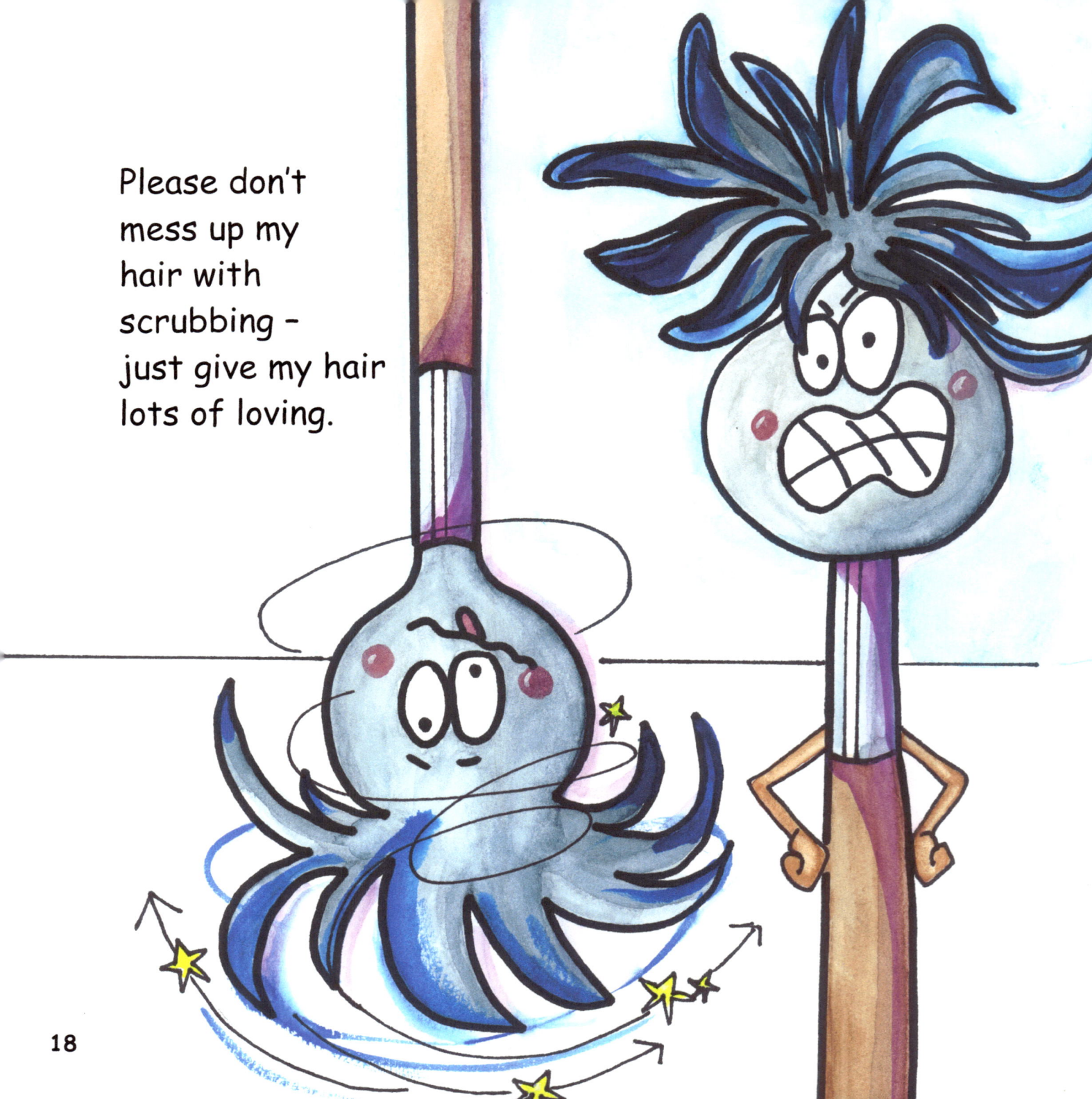

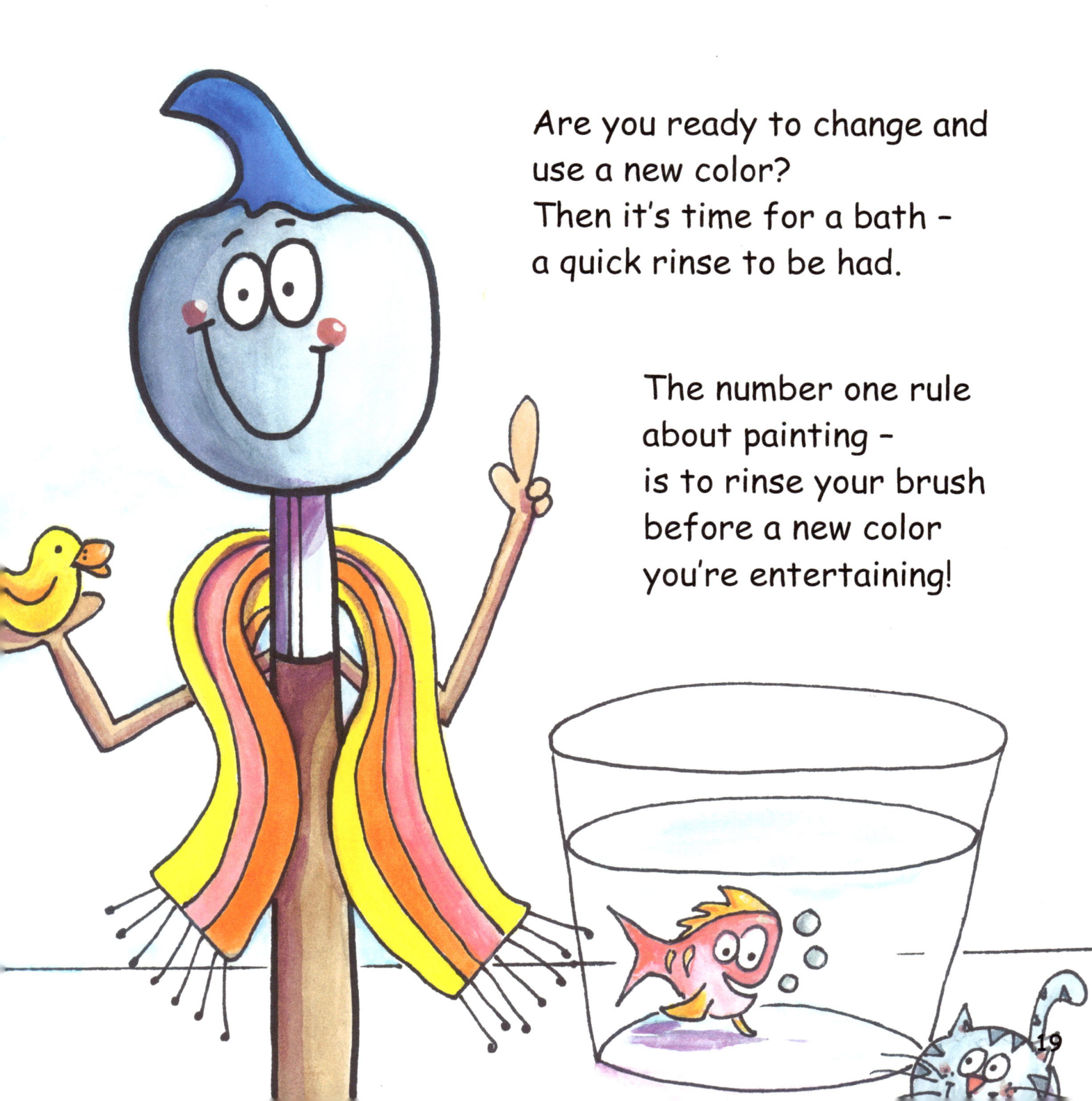

Are you ready to change and
use a new color?
Then it's time for a bath –
a quick rinse to be had.

The number one rule
about painting –
is to rinse your brush
before a new color
you're entertaining!

19

Into the bath I go,
round and round
I can feel the flow,
till my hair is clean and
ready to glow!

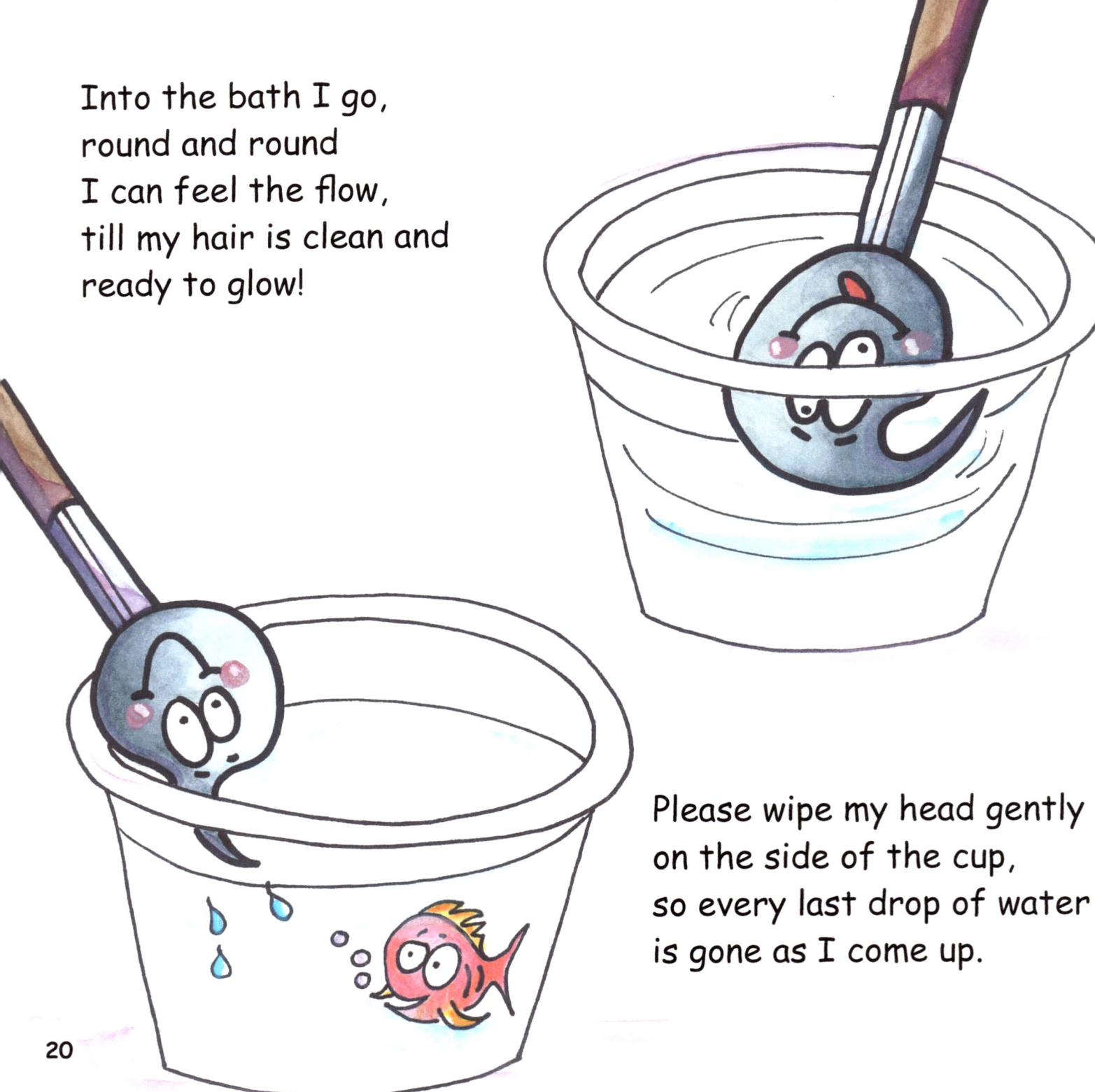

Please wipe my head gently
on the side of the cup,
so every last drop of water
is gone as I come up.

S'il vous plaît!!!
Please, don't bang my head
on the side of the cup,
for it makes my head ache
and splashes water –
for goodness sake!

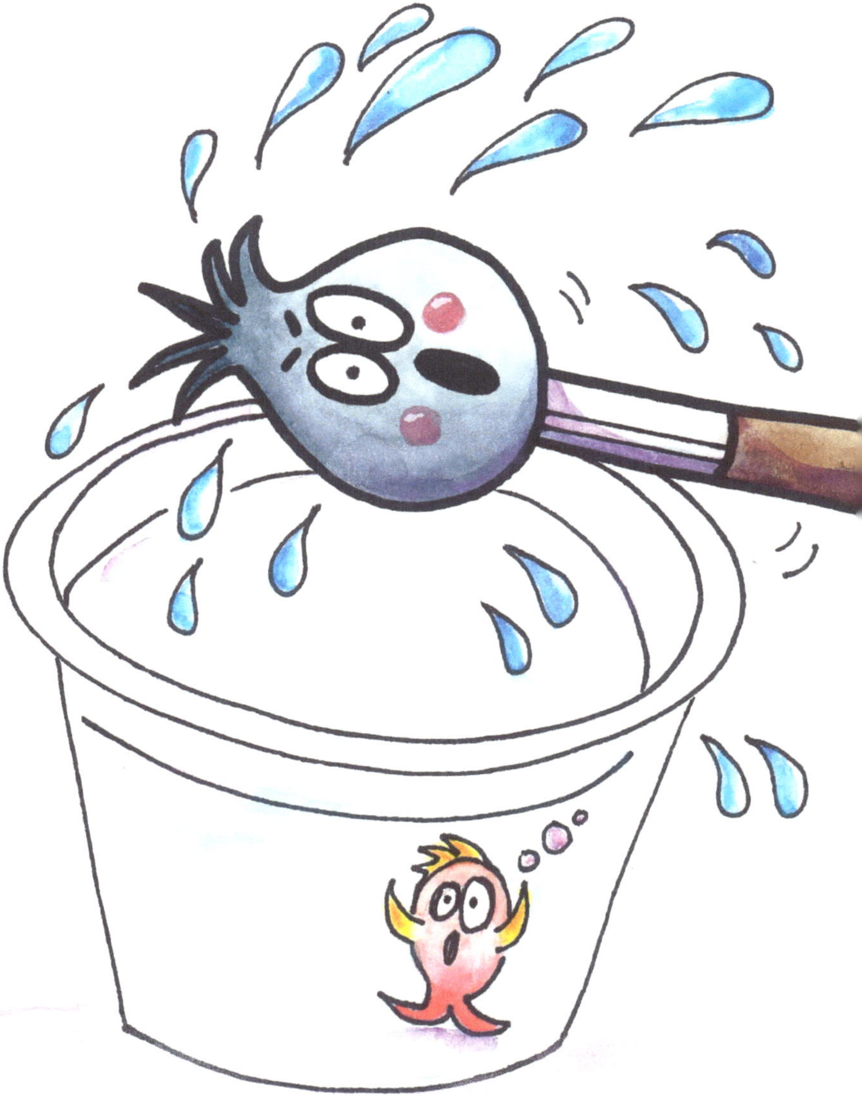

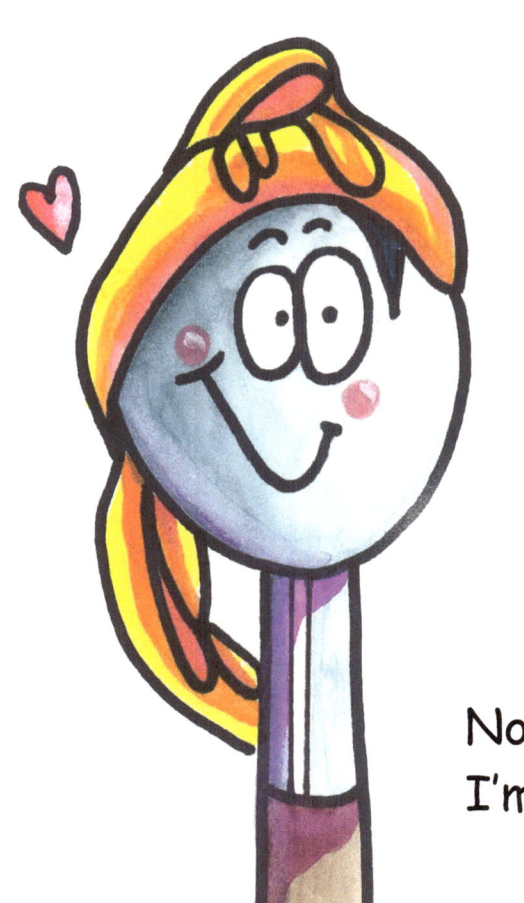

Now wipe my hair in a towel to dry,
I'm then ready for a new color to try!

If you want to mix a new color – that's great!
Don't do that in the jar or set,
please use a palette or a paper plate!

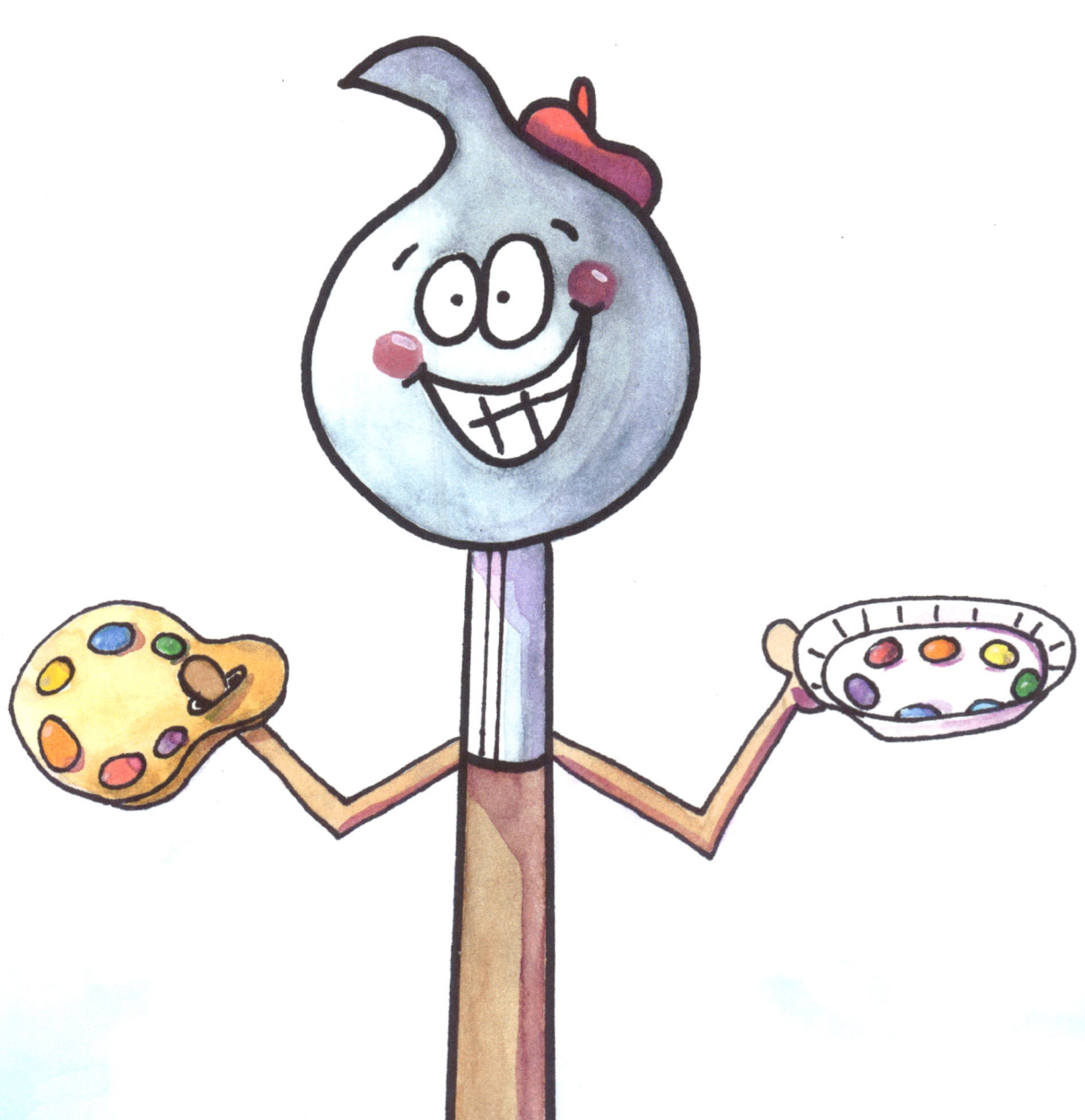

If you don't –
a big brown mess
is what you will have,
not the bright,
beautiful colors
that you wish
you had.

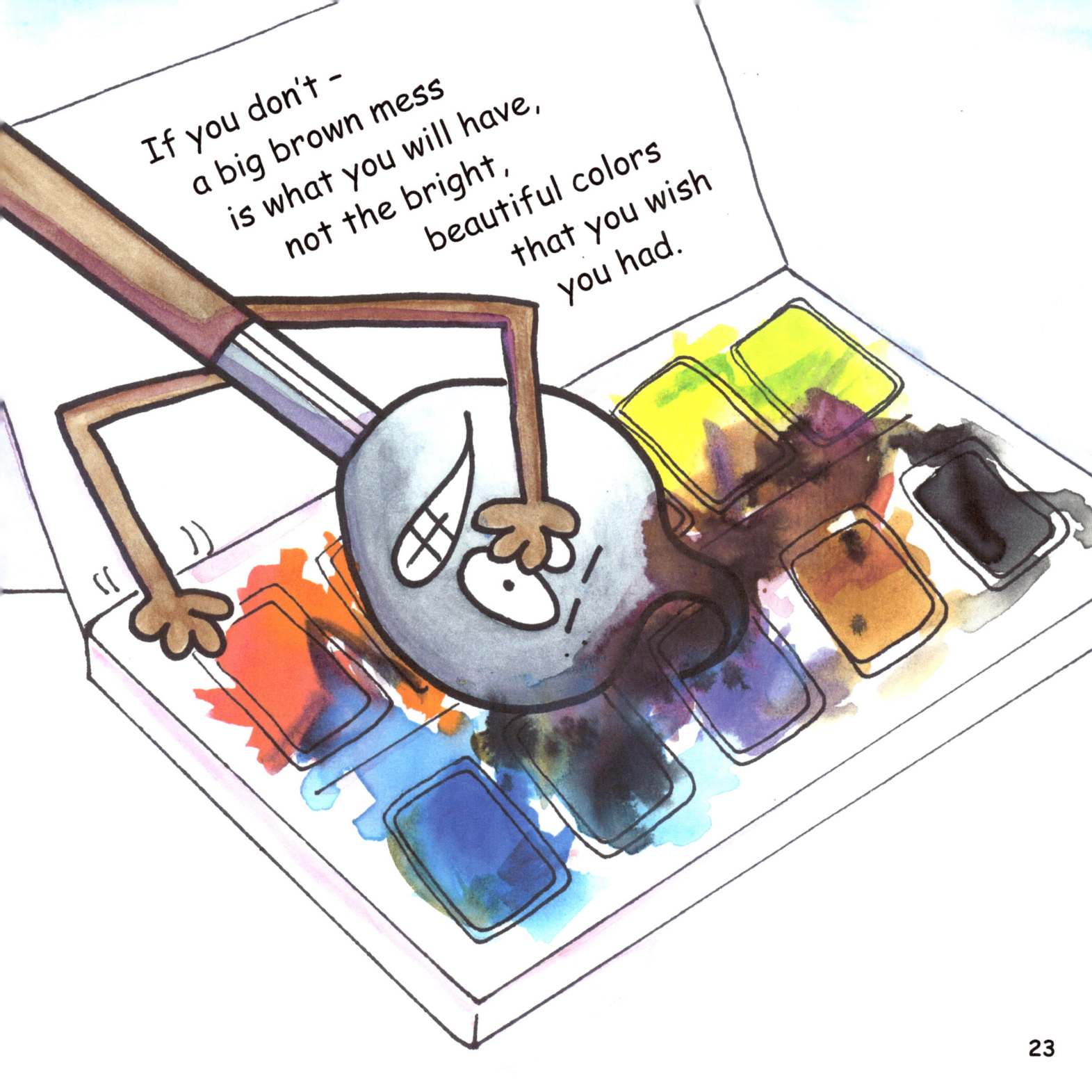

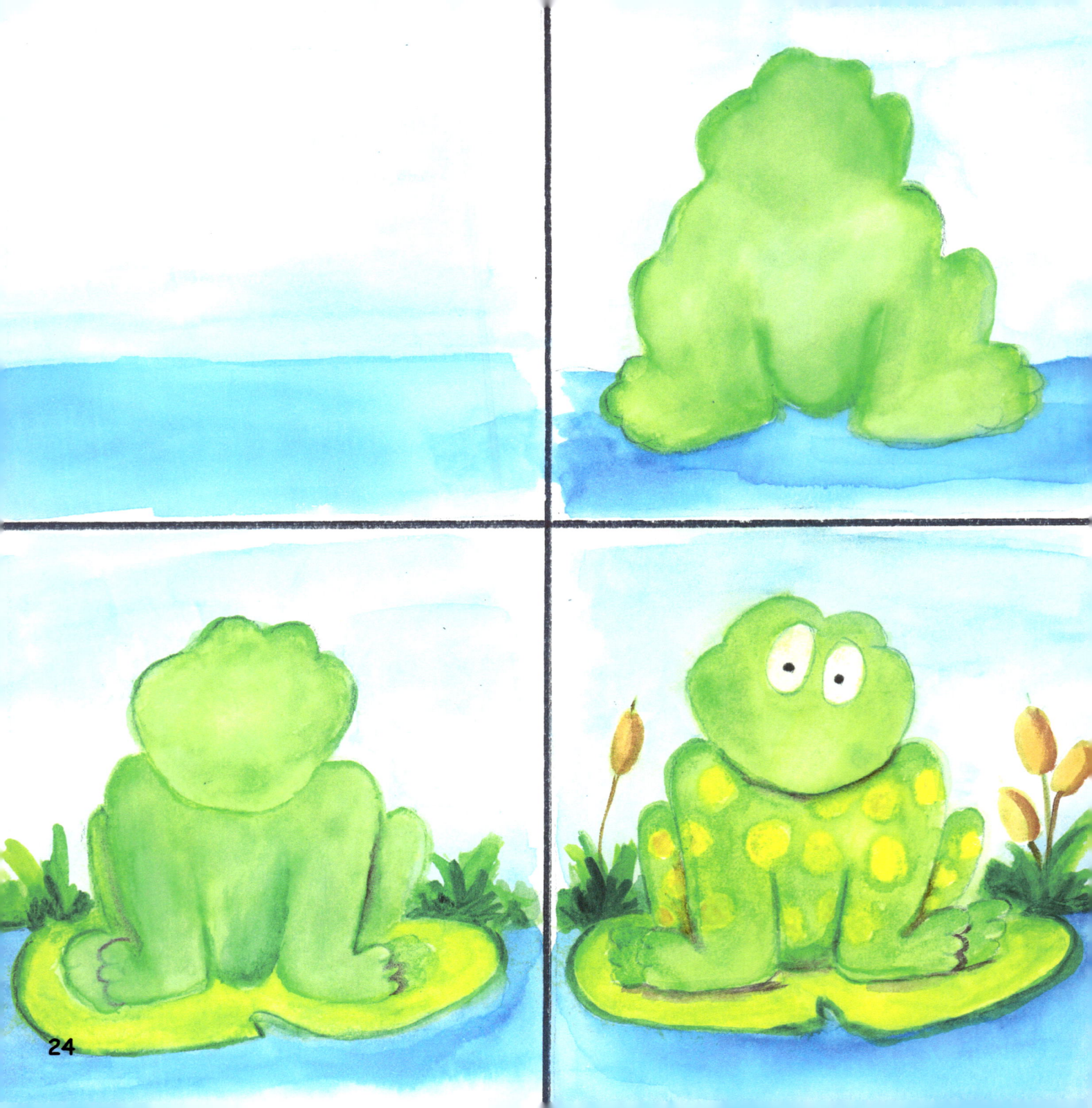

24

I think we are done – our painting is complete,
it's time to clean up and give my hair a treat!

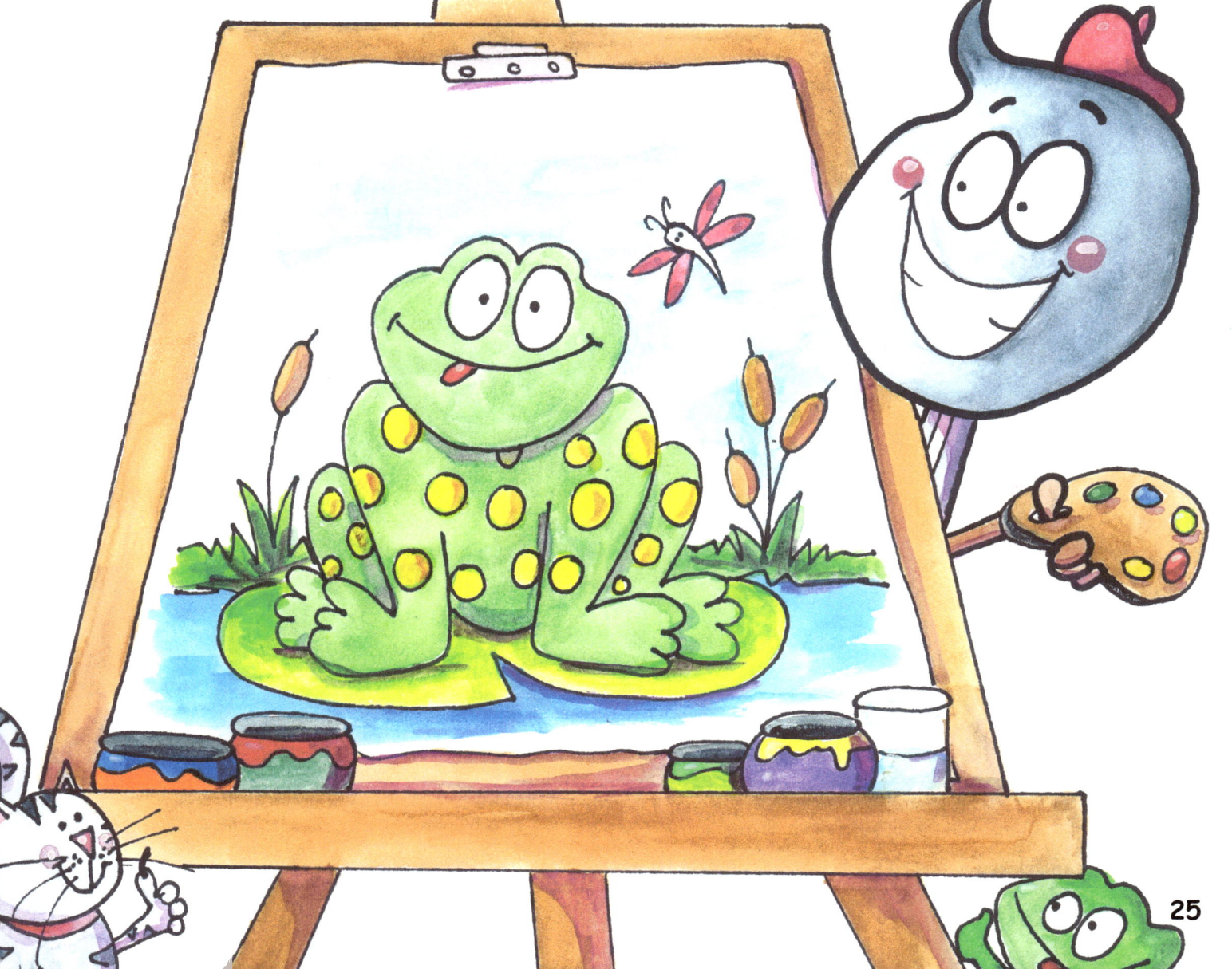

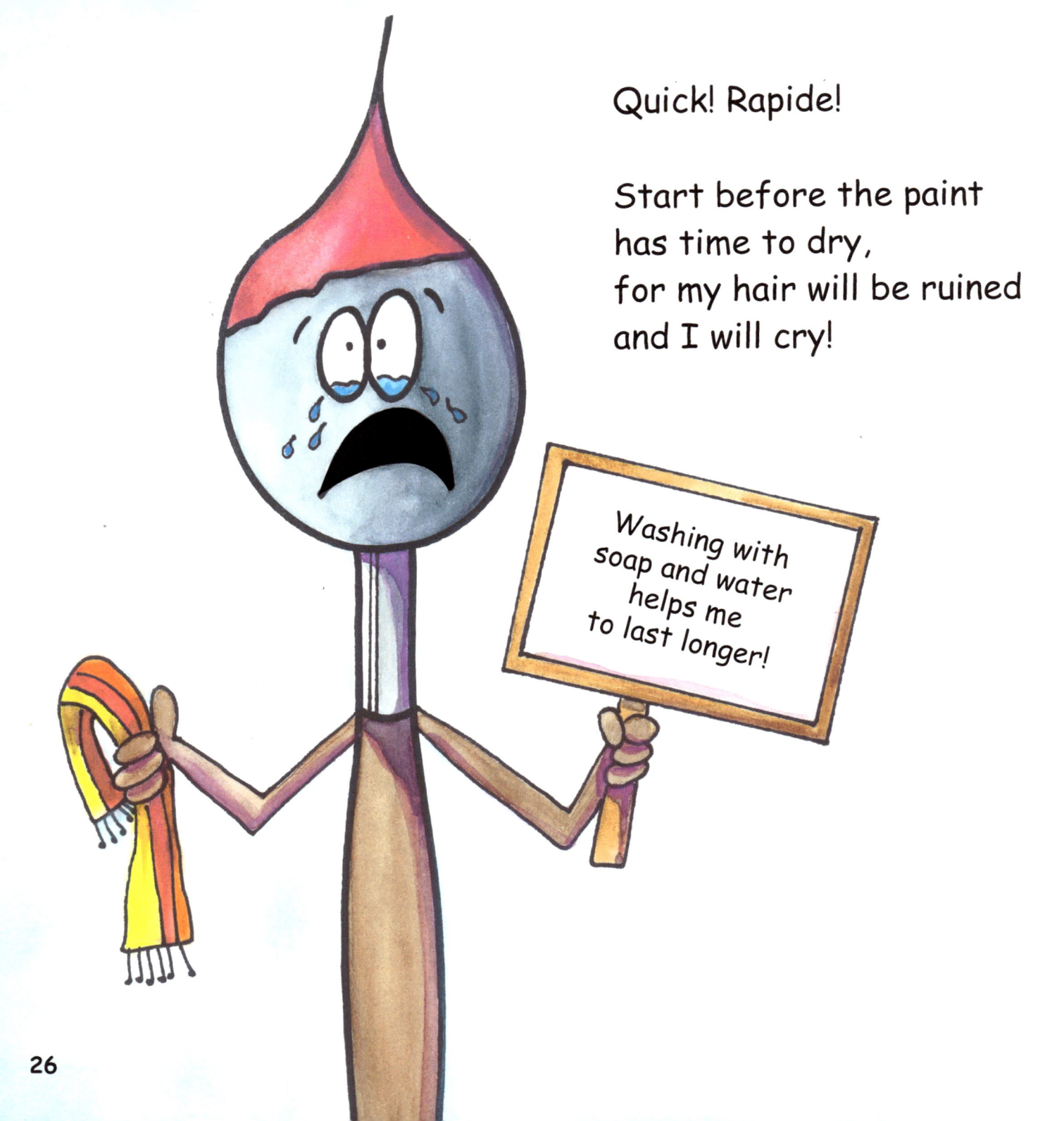

Quick! Rapide!

Start before the paint
has time to dry,
for my hair will be ruined
and I will cry!

Washing with
soap and water
helps me
to last longer!

26

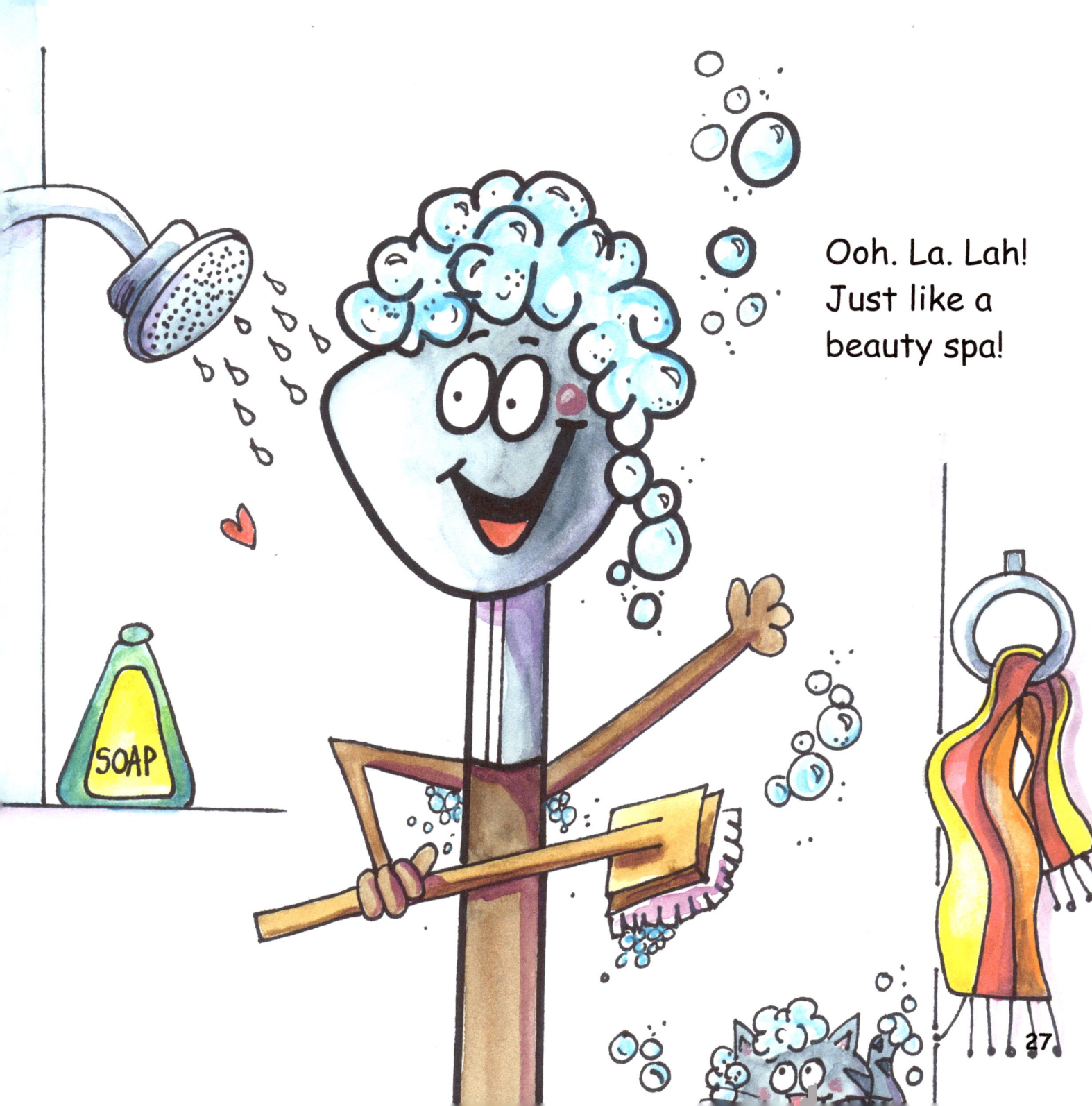

Ooh. La. Lah!
Just like a
beauty spa!

27

Now straighten my hair
so that it's nice and neat,
then stand me up tall on my feet.

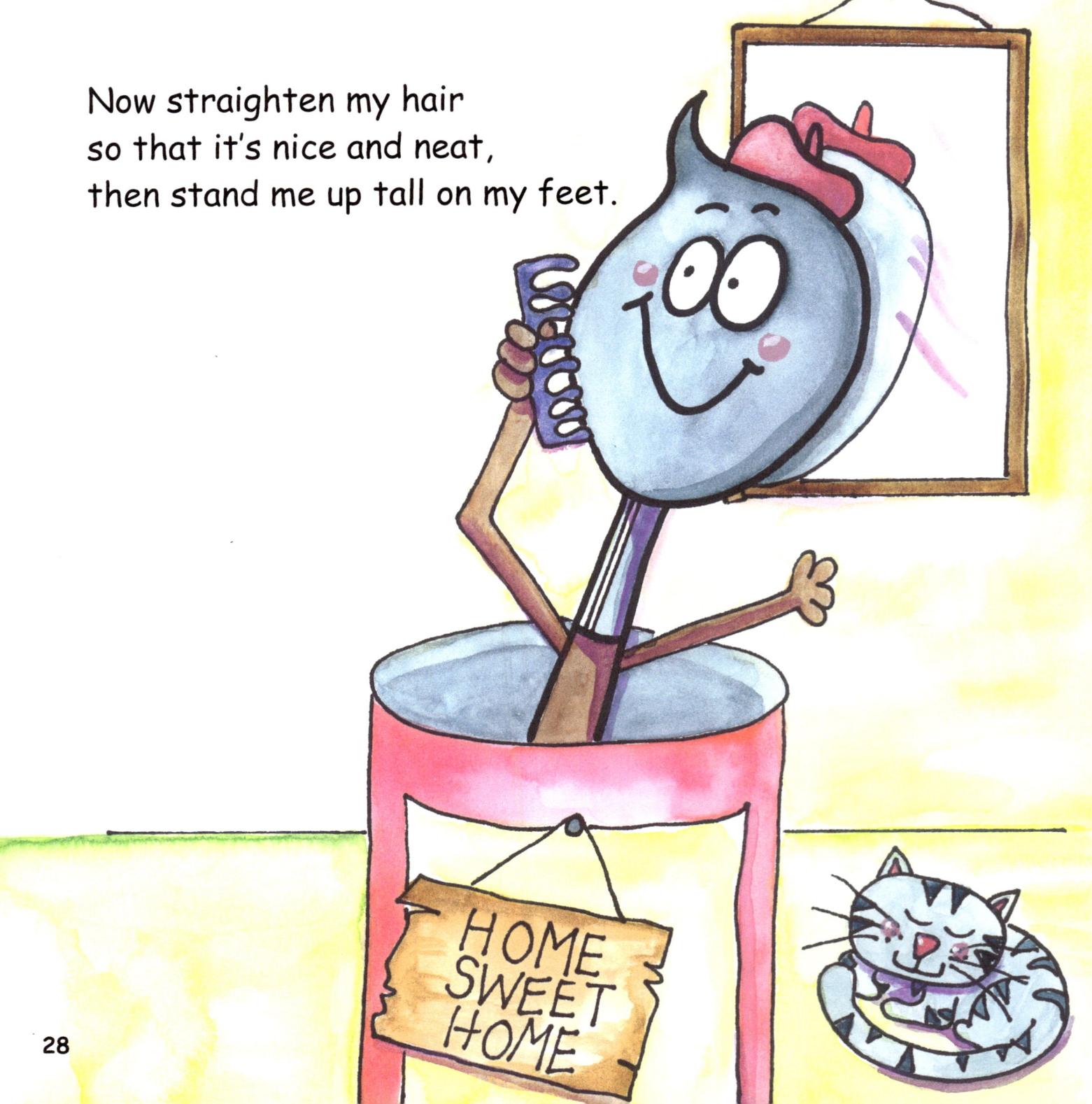

It's time to rest and get ready for bed.
 Don't store me face down – smashed on my head!

For my hair will be bent
 and I, Pierré,
  won't be worth a cent!

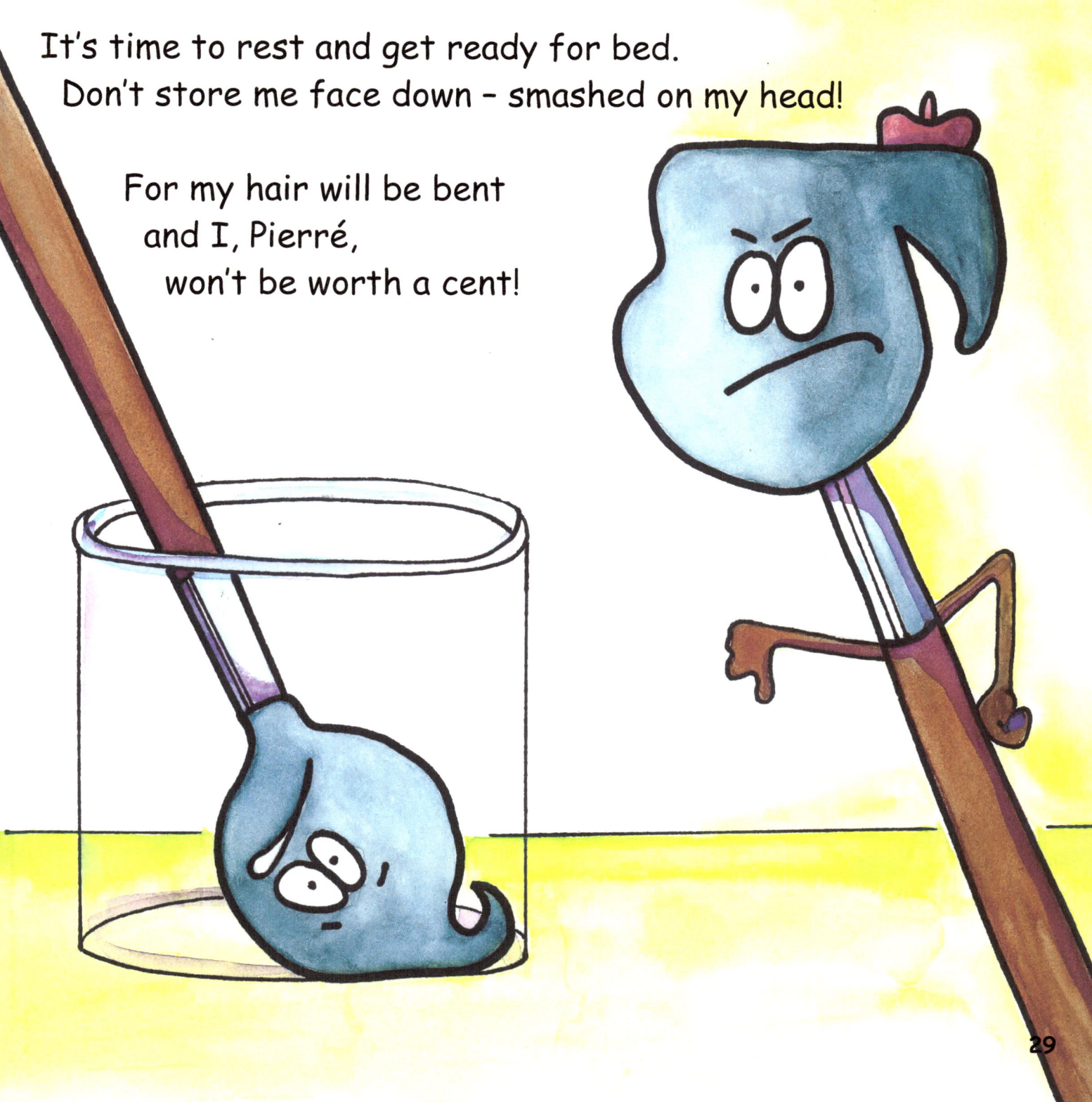

I hope you enjoyed painting with me,
I am a great friend to have, you see.
There are more paintings to paint –
yes, plenty there are
I hope to see you again my friend –

Au revoir'!

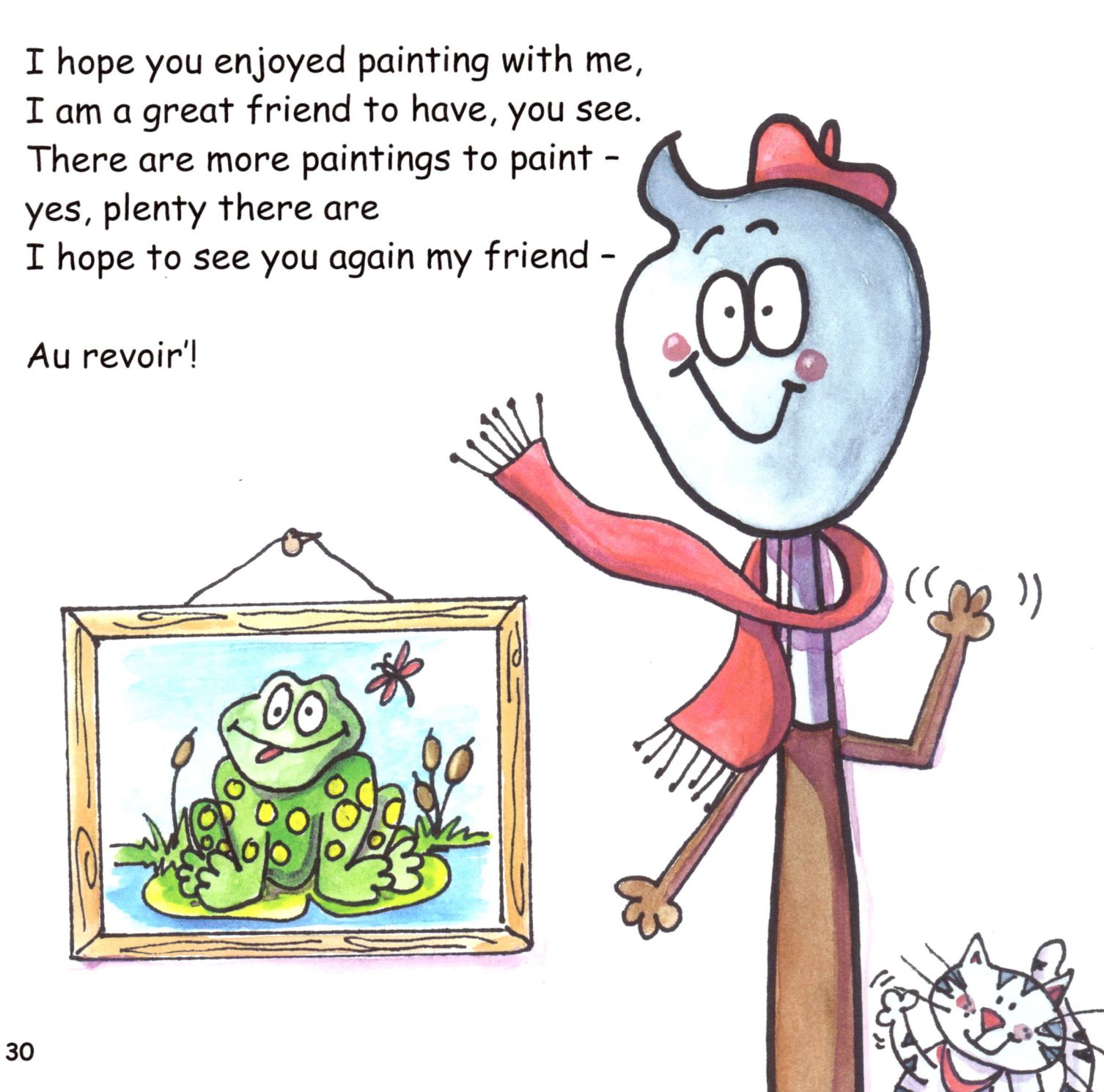

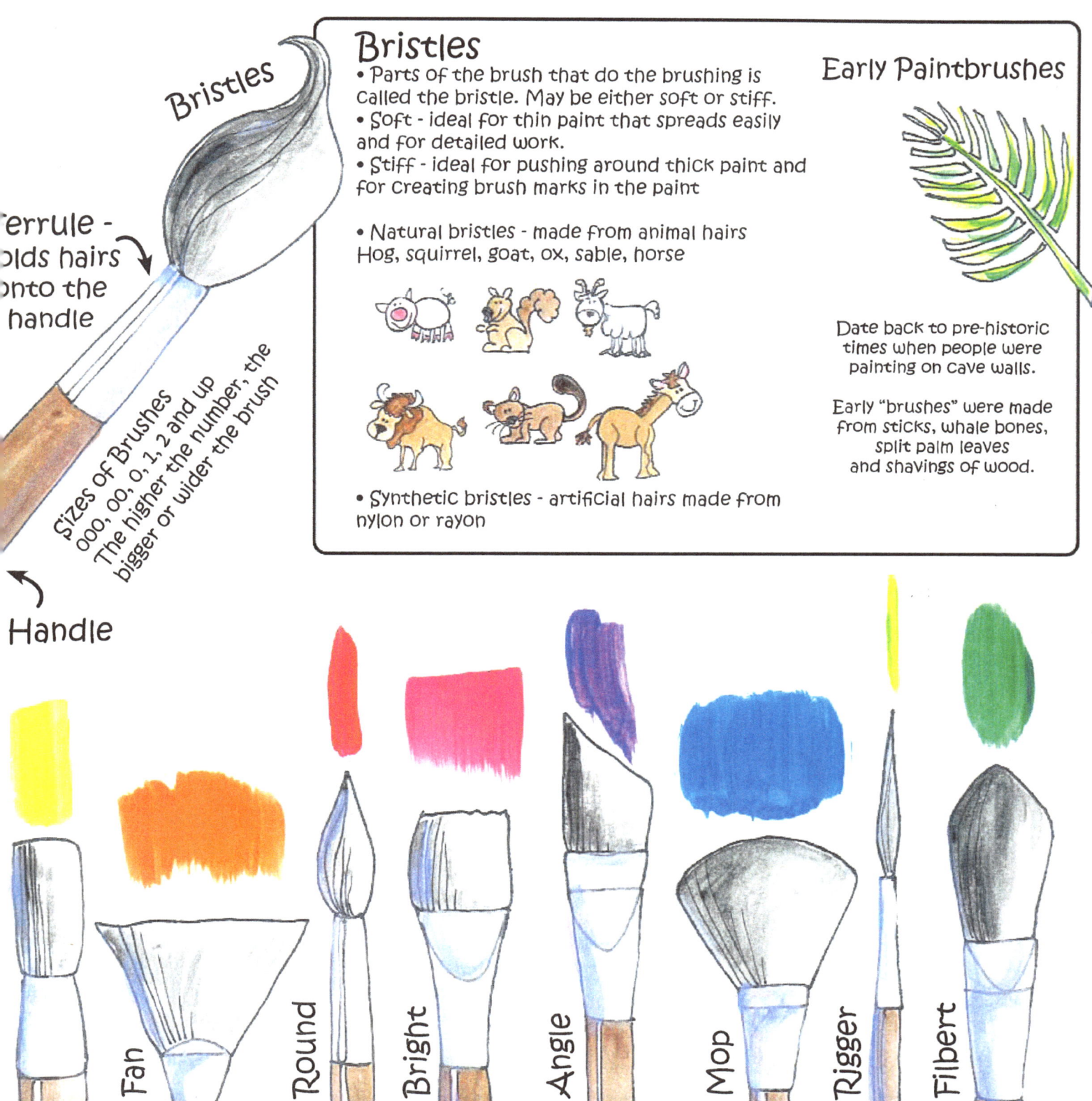

Bristles

Ferrule - holds hairs onto the handle

Sizes of Brushes
000, 00, 0, 1, 2 and up
The higher the number, the bigger or wider the brush

Handle

Bristles

- Parts of the brush that do the brushing is called the bristle. May be either soft or stiff.
- Soft - ideal for thin paint that spreads easily and for detailed work.
- Stiff - ideal for pushing around thick paint and for creating brush marks in the paint

- Natural bristles - made from animal hairs
Hog, squirrel, goat, ox, sable, horse

- Synthetic bristles - artificial hairs made from nylon or rayon

Early Paintbrushes

Date back to pre-historic times when people were painting on cave walls.

Early "brushes" were made from sticks, whale bones, split palm leaves and shavings of wood.

Fan   Round   Bright   Angle   Mop   Rigger   Filbert

French Translations

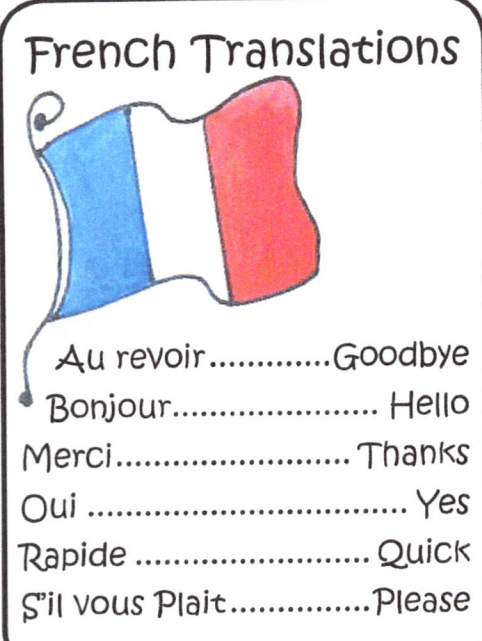

Au revoir.............Goodbye

Bonjour.....................Hello

Merci.......................Thanks

Oui ....Yes

Rapide ....Quick

S'il vous Plait...............Please

Try Painting With...

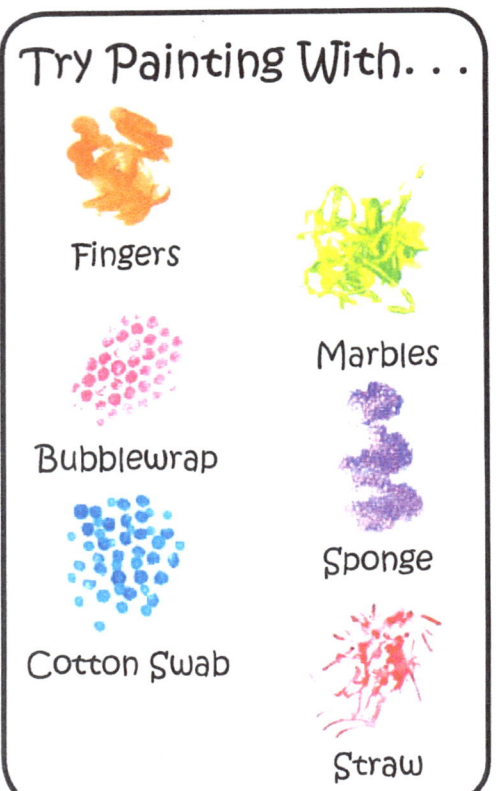

Fingers

Marbles

Bubblewrap

Sponge

Cotton Swab

Straw

Paper

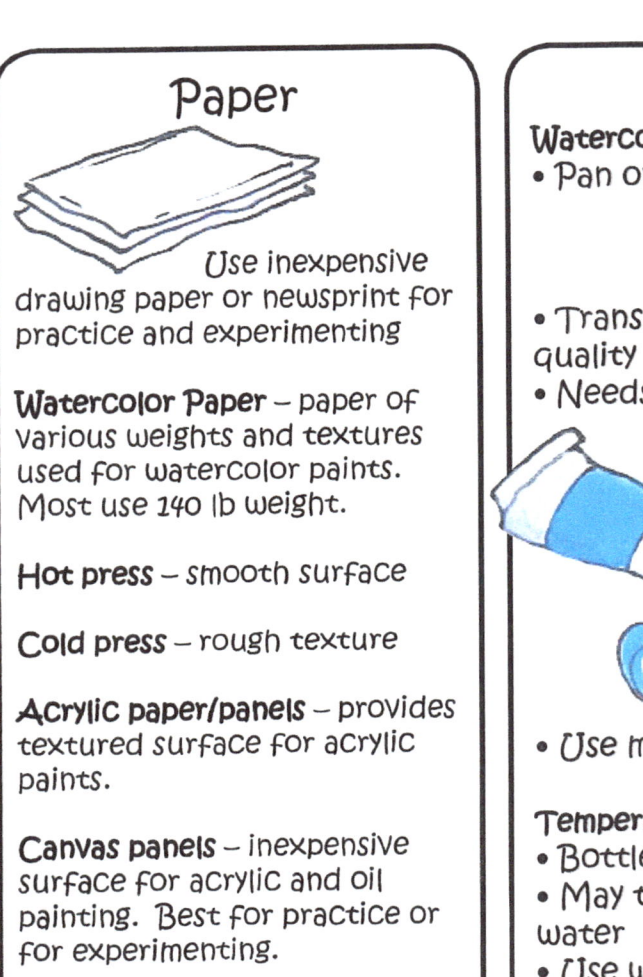

Use inexpensive drawing paper or newsprint for practice and experimenting

Watercolor Paper – paper of various weights and textures used for watercolor paints. Most use 140 lb weight.

Hot press – smooth surface

Cold press – rough texture

Acrylic paper/panels – provides textured surface for acrylic paints.

Canvas panels – inexpensive surface for acrylic and oil painting. Best for practice or for experimenting.

Stretched Canvas – best for oil and acrylic painting. Use for long term presentation.

Gesso – a priming material used on surfaces (canvas, linen, board) to prepare area for oil and acrylic painting.

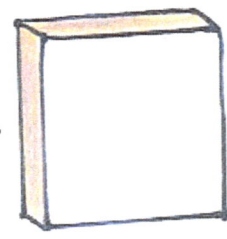

Paints

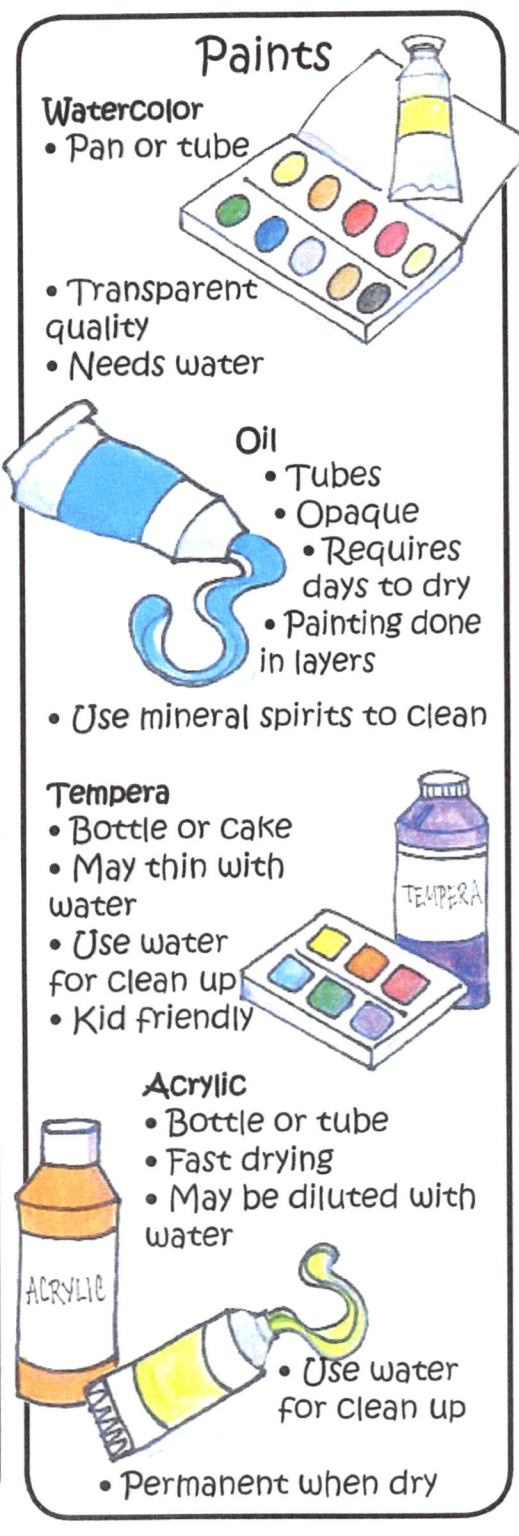

Watercolor
- Pan or tube
- Transparent quality
- Needs water

Oil
- Tubes
- Opaque
- Requires days to dry
- Painting done in layers
- Use mineral spirits to clean

Tempera
- Bottle or cake
- May thin with water
- Use water for clean up
- Kid friendly

Acrylic
- Bottle or tube
- Fast drying
- May be diluted with water
- Use water for clean up
- Permanent when dry

www.ingramcontent.com/pod-product-compliance
Lightning Source LLC
Chambersburg PA
CBHW050406180526
45159CB00005B/2170